SIGNS OF THE SECOND COMING

SIGNS OF THE SECOND COMING

11 REASONS JESUS WILL RETURN IN OUR LIFETIME

Britt Gillette

DEDICATION

To Samantha and Tommy.
May you always follow Jesus.

CONTENTS

Dedication v

Foreword 1

Chapter 1: The Timing of the Second Coming. 5

Chapter 2: The Nature of the Second Coming. 9

Chapter 3: The Exponential Curve 21

Chapter 4: Travel and Knowledge 35

Chapter 5: Israel 43

Chapter 6: Jerusalem 55

Chapter 7: Israel's Neighbors 61

Chapter 8: Gog of Magog 69

Chapter 9: Rome Revived. 77

Chapter 10: Global Government. 87

Chapter 11: Advanced Technology. 93

Chapter 12: Worldwide Preaching of The Gospel 101

Chapter 13: Convergence 107

Chapter 14: Why Does it Matter?. 123

Chapter 15: He's Coming!. 131

About the Author 137

FOREWORD

IN MY FIRST BOOK, *Coming To Jesus: One Man's Search for Truth and Life Purpose*, I tell the story of my personal struggle with the universal questions of life and my search to uncover the truth. That search ultimately led to the Bible, where I discovered the existence of countless specific and fulfilled prophecies.

In my mind, the existence of these prophecies verifies the claim that the Bible is the Word of God. No other book in the history of the world comes anywhere close to matching the Bible's track record of fulfilled prophecy. In fact, if you're keeping score (and you should), the Bible has a ***perfect*** track record when it comes to fulfilled prophecy. That's right. Perfect.

Every single prophecy found in the Bible (with the exception of those regarding the end times and beyond) has been fulfilled to the last letter. Did you know that? Years ago, I didn't. But then I discovered these astounding prophecies – detailed prophecies written hundreds and sometimes thousands of years in advance.

For example, did you know the Bible foretold the rise of the Greek Empire under Alexander the Great and its break-up into four kingdoms following his death (***Daniel 8:5-22***)? Did you know the Bible foretold the destruction of the Temple and the long, worldwide exile of the Jewish people (***Luke 21:20-24***)? The Bible even called out Cyrus the Great by name as the king who would give the command to rebuild Jerusalem and the Temple (***Isaiah 44:28-45:13***). And the Bible made every one of these prophecies centuries in advance of their fulfillment. But you know what else?

That's just the tip of the iceberg.

THE MESSIANIC PROPHECIES

The Bible also foretold the coming of a Messiah who would save the world. The prophet Zechariah claimed He would release a multitude from "death in a waterless dungeon" (*Zechariah 9:11*). And the prophet Isaiah said, through Him, many will be counted as righteous (*Isaiah 53:11-12*). The Messianic prophecies are so specific and detailed in nature, they even include the actual year of the Messiah's arrival foretold more than 400 years in advance (*Daniel 9:25*). They detail the His birth, life, death, and resurrection, and these prophecies were all fulfilled in the life of one man and one man only – Jesus of Nazareth.

In fact, these prophecies played a pivotal role in my commitment to follow Jesus. But of course, if you read my first book, you know this already. But you know what?

That's not all I found...

Yet To Be Fulfilled Prophecies

Through study of the Bible, I found something else – hundreds of prophecies concerning *future* events. So what are these prophecies about? A whole range of subjects such as future wars, political events, and the establishment of an everlasting Kingdom ruled by Jesus Himself. But an overwhelming number of these prophecies focus on a single event – the Second Coming of Jesus Christ. In fact, the Bible contains more prophecies describing His Second Coming than it does His First.

Given that every single prophecy describing His First Coming was fulfilled to the letter, doesn't it make sense to believe the prophecies of His Second Coming will also be fulfilled? I think so. In my mind, the only question is *when* they will be fulfilled, not *if.*

Watching for Signs

Jesus rebuked the religious elites of His day for their failure to recognize His First Coming. He told them, "You know how to look at the sky and predict the weather, but you don't know how to recognize the signs of the times" (*Matthew 16:1-3*). In other words, just like you and me, the Pharisees and Sadducees could look at dark clouds on the horizon and know that a rain storm was on its way. Likewise, they also knew the Old Testament Messianic prophecies. Yet they failed to recognize their fulfillment in Jesus. Had they prepared themselves spiritually and made a serious commitment to study the Messianic prophecies and watch for their fulfillment, I have no doubt they would have recognized Jesus as the Messiah.

But there's more to this story. As I studied the Bible, I realized Jesus wasn't simply addressing the Pharisees and Sadducees. He had a second audience in mind. Who?

You and me.

That's right. Jesus was talking to you and me. Jesus had a lot to say about His return, and He told us to faithfully watch for it. In fact, He did far more than that. He ***commanded*** us to watch:

> *"You, too, must keep watch! For you don't know when the master of the household will return – in the evening, at midnight, before dawn, or at daybreak. Don't let him find you sleeping when he arrives without warning. I say to you what I say to everyone: Watch for him!"* ***Mark 13:35-37*** *(NLT)*

As a follower of Jesus, I take this command seriously. And long ago, I made a conscious decision to stay alert, study these signs, and watch as He commanded. But what I found when I studied these prophecies is not at all what I expected. What did I find? I found that all the signs Jesus and the prophets said to look for are present ***right now***.

And not only are they present, but ours is the only generation in all of history that can make that claim. And you know what else? Jesus said once you see the presence of all those signs, He's coming. Does that get your attention?

CHAPTER 1

THE TIMING OF THE SECOND COMING

ON OCTOBER 22, 1844, thousands of people throughout the United States gathered on hills and mountain tops. Many of them sold everything they owned in anticipation of that day. Some left their jobs. Others even left their families. But why? What did those people gather together and do on those hills and mountaintops?

Believe it or not, they waited. That's right. They waited. All day long, they sat around and waited. But why?

They waited because they had convinced themselves beyond all doubt that October 22, 1844 was the day of the Second Coming of Jesus Christ. You've probably heard of this group.

Their belief was based in part on the teachings of William Miller. A Baptist preacher, Miller originally pinpointed the date of the Second Coming as destined to occur sometime between March 1843 and March 1844.

When those dates came and went, most of his followers (known as Millerites) realized the error of their ways and returned to life as normal. But the rest latched onto a new date and gathered together on that infamous Tuesday in 1844. Needless to say, the result was the same. That date too came and went, and Jesus did not return.

So why am I telling you this story? Because I want you to know that the Millerites should have known without a doubt that October 22, 1844 was ***not*** the day of Jesus' return. Why? Because Jesus Himself said "no man knows the day or the hour of my return, not even myself. Only my Father in heaven knows" (***Mark 13:32***). So any attempt to set a specific date for the Second Coming is nothing more than pure guesswork. It's completely at odds with God's Word.

THE NEGATIVE EFFECTS OF DATE SETTING

Even though Jesus made it clear that no one can know the day or the hour of His return, that hasn't stopped an untold number of people from claiming He will return on a specific date. One modern example is the media circus surrounding Harold Camping's prediction that Jesus would return on May 21, 2011. Of course, you and I both know Jesus didn't come back that day.

Nevertheless, Camping and the Millerites are far from an isolated case when it comes to the practice of "date setting." History is littered with individuals and groups who preached Jesus would return on a specific day or at a specific time. Yet every one of those claims ended in disappointment.

It's bad enough when false predictions shake the faith of a few misguided people, but date setting has had a much more devastating effect. So many people have sounded false alarms that any mention of the Second Coming falls on deaf ears. It's like a modern day case of *The Boy Who Cried Wolf*.

Because of date setters, many people (and that includes a lot of Christians) have simply written off the prospect that Jesus will ***ever*** return, while others heap scorn and ridicule on those who look forward to His Coming.

Today, anyone who dares to suggest the Second Coming of Jesus Christ might take place any time in the near future is mocked and ridiculed. A common refrain we often hear from skeptics goes something like this, "*Jesus is coming? Sure. Heard that one before. So and so claimed Jesus was coming in the year 1000. Didn't happen. So and so claimed He was coming in 1790 and 1844 and 1900 and 2000, etc. Every single one of those claims was wrong, and anyone who says He's coming back now will be just as wrong.*"

Now, I can understand why a lot of people feel this way. After all, on the face of it, this argument seems to make sense. But there's a big problem with it. It attributes failed human predictions to the Bible – predictions the

Bible didn't make. After all, the Bible didn't predict the return of Jesus Christ in 1844 – the Millerites did. The Bible didn't predict that Y2K would herald the Second Coming – imperfect humans did.

If you take the time to examine the evidence, you'll find it's not the Bible that has a history of failed predictions. It's people. In contrast, the Bible's track record is **perfect**. And in regard to the Second Coming, it's clear about what we should look for.

THE TIME OF HIS COMING

So if Jesus Himself says no one can know the day or the hour of His Coming, what (if anything) can we know about it? For years, I've heard people say we can't know anything at all. Yet, that's far from what Jesus said. So why is it that so many Christians insist we can't know anything about the timing of His return? What is their belief based on?

More often than not, their belief is based on the idea that Jesus "will come like a thief in the night" (*1 Thessalonians 5:2*), and this is true. Jesus Himself said He would come like a thief in the night "when least expected" (*Matthew 24:43-44*).

This idea, coupled with the statement that "no one can know the day or the hour" of His return, has led many people to conclude that no one can know anything about when Jesus is coming. After all, if He comes like a thief in the night when least expected, how could you know when He's coming?

That's a good question. And fortunately, I know the answer. You see, I've read the Bible, and it clearly tells us that we can know the general "season" of His return. Don't believe me? Just read the rest of Paul's letter to the Thessalonians.

While it says Jesus will come like a thief in the night when least expected, it also says **Christians will not be surprised**. Here's the full context of that passage (emphasis mine):

> *"But you aren't in the dark about these things, dear brothers and sisters, and **you won't be surprised when the day of the***

Lord comes like a thief. For you are all children of the light and of the day; we don't belong to darkness and night. So be on your guard, not asleep like the others. Stay alert and be clearheaded. Night is the time when people sleep and drinkers get drunk. But let us who live in the light be clearheaded, protected by the armor of faith and love, and wearing as our helmet the confidence of our salvation."   **1 Thessalonians 5:4-8 (NLT)**

Did you catch that? Do you see what this passage says? It says that Jesus will come like a thief in the night and surprise non-Christians and Christians who are spiritually asleep. Alert and watchful Christians will not be caught off guard by His return. But how can this be?

While Jesus said we can never know **the day or the hour** of His return (**Matthew 24:36**), we do have the ability to recognize the **general timeframe**. Why do I say this?

Because that's what Jesus Himself said.

When His disciples asked Him to describe "the signs of His coming," Jesus described a number of events and concluded by saying, "When you see these things occur, look up. For your salvation is near!" (**Luke 21:28**).

Is Jesus contradicting Himself? After all, in one instance, Jesus tells us no one can know the day or the hour of His return. Then later, He says we should look up for Him when we see certain events occur. On the face of it, this doesn't make sense. So how do we reconcile these statements? The answer is by reading and understanding God's Word. After all, the Bible clearly states what will happen in the last days.

So what does it say about the Second Coming? Does the Bible say we can know the time of Christ's return? The answer might surprise you. Because it's both yes **and** no.

Now when I say that, you're probably thinking, *"Now wait a minute, Britt. You can't straddle the fence on this one. It's either one or the other. It can't be both!"* But I assure you that's not the case. The Bible is quite clear. But in order to grasp this concept, you first need to understand **the nature** of the Second Coming.

CHAPTER 2
THE NATURE OF THE SECOND COMING

THERE'S A STORY in the Book of Matthew where Jesus explains to His disciples that He must go to Jerusalem, suffer at the hands of the priests and religious teachers of the law, be executed, and rise on the third day. But when Peter heard this, he found it hard to believe. He took Jesus aside and essentially told him, "Stop talking this way. Certainly this won't happen to you!" Jesus replied in a sharp tone saying, "Away from me Satan! You see things only from your human point of view and not from God's" (*Matthew 16:21-23*).

Sounds harsh, doesn't it? But can you see why Jesus responded this way? With the benefit of hindsight, we can see what Peter did not. Without the crucifixion and the resurrection of Jesus Christ, we're condemned to die in our sins. Redemption? Impossible. Hope? There wouldn't be any. To die for the sins of the world is the whole reason Jesus came. So why did Peter rebuke Him for it?

The answer is clear when you put yourself in the shoes of a 1st Century Israelite. Before the crucifixion, Peter and the other apostles had a far different view of Jesus than they did later in life. At that time, the Jewish people eagerly anticipated the coming of God's Messiah – a man they believed would conquer their Roman oppressors and establish a worldwide everlasting physical kingdom of justice and righteousness.

Peter and his fellow apostles looked at Jesus, and they didn't see a man destined for crucifixion. Instead, they saw Daniel's prophesied Messiah – the one given authority over the whole world, whose rule is eternal and whose kingdom is never-ending (*Daniel 7:14*). They weren't wrong to think this.

Jesus confirmed He was Daniel's prophesied ruler when He told the high priest that he would see "the son of man at the right hand of God coming on the clouds of heaven" (*Mark 14:62*). The problem is that Jesus referred to a future event, while the apostles expected fulfillment in their day and time.

But why did they expect this? Where did they go wrong? The mistake came when they failed to recognize *the nature* of His Coming. And what did they fail to see? That the Messiah would come twice. First as a suffering Servant offered as a blood sacrifice for the sins of the world (*Isaiah 53*), and second as a conquering King who would establish an everlasting Kingdom (*Daniel 7*). Both sets of prophecies point to Jesus, but Peter and the apostles had the cart before the horse. Before setting up His everlasting Kingdom, Jesus came first to save the world.

WHEN HISTORY REPEATS ITSELF

Like Peter, many Christians today have a similar misconception – not about the First Coming, but about the Second Coming of Jesus Christ. And just like His First Coming, you can't understand the Second Coming unless you first understand its nature. Why? Because before you can understand *when* it will happen, you need to understand *how* it will happen.

So what is this misconception? It's the same as the first one – the Messiah will come twice. Don't believe me? Go ahead and read these two passages in the Bible:

> *"We who are still living when the Lord returns will not meet him ahead of those who have died. For the Lord himself will come down from heaven with a commanding shout, with the voice of the archangel, and with the trumpet call of God. First, the Christians who have died will rise from their graves. Then,*

together with them, we who are still alive and remain on the earth will be caught up in the clouds to meet the Lord in the air. Then we will be with the Lord forever. So encourage each other with these words." **1 Thessalonians 4:15-18** *(NLT)*

"Then I saw heaven opened, and a white horse was standing there. Its rider was named Faithful and True, for he judges fairly and wages a righteous war. His eyes were like flames of fire, and on his head were many crowns. A name was written on him that no one understood except himself. He wore a robe dipped in blood, and his title was the Word of God. The armies of heaven, dressed in the finest of pure white linen, followed him on white horses. From his mouth came a sharp sword to strike down the nations. He will rule them with an iron rod. He will release the fierce wrath of God, the Almighty, like juice flowing from a winepress. On his robe at his thigh was written this title: King of all kings and Lord of all lords." **Revelation 19:11-16** *(NLT)*

Both these passages describe the physical return of Jesus Christ. But they also describe two dramatically different depictions of His return. Why? There can only be one reason. They describe two entirely different events. In other words, as we approach the end of the age, Jesus will return twice. So let's take a look at how the Bible describes these two distinct events.

THE RAPTURE

Sometime in the future, Jesus will come down from heaven and meet Christians in the air – both the living and the dead. He won't actually set foot on the earth, but will gather believers together in the clouds with a shout and the sound of a trumpet (*1 Thessalonians 4:16-17*). This is called the rapture, and it will happen in a mere moment – in the blink of an eye.

If you're a believer when this happens, you'll see your body transformed from the dying mortal body you have now to a glorious, eternal body (*1*

Corinthians 15:51-52). This new body will be just like the glorious resurrected body of Jesus (*Philippians 3:21*). If you're not a believer, you'll remain on the earth and nothing will happen to your body. In fact, if not for some missing people, it's unlikely you'll notice anything happened at all.

When the rapture occurs, Jesus will **not** set up His eternal Kingdom on earth. Instead, He will take believers back to heaven where He has prepared a place for them (*John 14:2-3*). This is in sharp contrast to the actual Second Coming which will occur at a later time.

THE SECOND COMING

When the Second Coming takes place, Jesus will return to earth as the Leader of Heaven's Armies. He will come on the clouds of heaven with great power and glory (*Matthew 24:30*). His coming will be seen by the whole world (*Colossians 3:4*), and there will be deep mourning among the people of the world, not joy (*Matthew 24:30*). He will physically set foot on the earth. In fact, His feet will stand on the Mount of Olives, and it will split in two (*Zechariah 14:4*). Instead of coming *for* His holy people, He will come *with* them (*1 Thessalonians 1:7-10*), and He will execute judgment on the world (*Jude 1:14-15*). He will fight against the Antichrist, the kings of the world, and their armies (*Revelation 19:18-19*), and He will destroy the Antichrist with the breath of His mouth and the glory of His coming (*2 Thessalonians 2:8*). In doing so, He will set up a kingdom that will never be destroyed (*Daniel 2:44*), and He will be given authority over all the nations of the world (*Daniel 7:13-14*).

THE RAPTURE VS. THE SECOND COMING

Can you see now why the return of Jesus confuses so many people? It's because He will come back twice. If you think both these events are one and the same, it's understandable you'll find it hard to reconcile the two accounts. This is the reason why some people claim Jesus will come unexpectedly while others claim He won't. It's the reason why some people claim He will meet believers in the clouds, while others claim He will come down to earth with an army of saints.

Both claims are true, and any confusion is simply the result of our failure to understand the differences between these two events. Both involve the return of Jesus, but they are not one and the same. This causes the same type of confusion Peter and the apostles experienced when they failed to recognize the distinction between the Messiah as a conquering King and the Messiah as a suffering Servant.

So clearly there are a number of differences between the rapture and the Second Coming. But what do we know about their timing?

THE TRIBULATION

Before we can fully understand the timing of these events, we must first understand an unprecedented time period described in the Bible. Both Jesus and Daniel call it, "a time of greater anguish than at any time since nations first came into existence" (***Matthew 24:21; Daniel 12:1***). Can you imagine that? Think of the horrors of World War II and the Holocaust. Can anything be worse than that? According to the Bible, the answer is yes.

In the Book of Revelation, John describes the events of the Tribulation, events which include tormenting locusts, a great earthquake, a rainstorm of hail and fire, the death of one-half of mankind, and other horrors.

This seven year period is referred to by most Christians as "the Tribulation." But the Bible uses many names, including "the time of Jacob's trouble," "the seventieth week of Daniel," and "the day of the Lord's vengeance."

There's a lot to know about the Tribulation. Entire books have been written about it and what it will bring. But for our purposes, two aspects are particularly relevant. First, it is a time when God will bring judgment upon the world. And second, it's marked by specific, identifiable events. Knowing these two key points will help you understand the timing of the rapture and the Second Coming.

CHAPTER 2

THE TIMING OF THE RAPTURE

Can we know the timing of the rapture? To find out, let's examine some of its characteristics. According to the Bible, the rapture is:

1. Not preceded by signs
2. Happens when life on earth is "business as usual," and
3. Occurs before the Tribulation

So let's take a look at each one.

NOT PRECEDED BY SIGNS

Nowhere in the Bible does it say the rapture will be preceded by any signs or events indicating that it's near. This is why so many people insist we can't know anything about the timing of Christ's return. It's because we can't – at least in regard to the rapture. The confusion comes when people read passages about the rapture and attribute them to the Second Coming. They then conclude that no one can know the timing of the Second Coming.

For example, Jesus tells a parable about a man who went on a long trip. But before he left, he gave each of his servants instructions on what to do. He told the gatekeeper to keep watch and stay ready for his return. He then said we too must keep watch, for we don't know when the master of the house will return. So don't be asleep when he *arrives without warning* (**Mark 13:34-36**). Jesus then commands us to watch for His return.

In the parable of the ten bridesmaids, Jesus tells the story of ten women with lamps who go out to meet the bridegroom. Five of them bring along extra oil for their lamps, while the remaining five are foolish and don't bring enough for their lamps. They soon leave to go buy more, and when they do, the bridegroom arrives. The five bridesmaids who remain enter with Him into the wedding feast, while the others are locked out. The lesson? Jesus says, "Keep watch! For you don't know the day or the hour of my return" (**Matthew 25:1-13**).

In both parables, Jesus tells us to be prepared for His return at all times. Why? Because without warning, the rapture could occur at any moment.

WHEN LIFE IS "BUSINESS AS USUAL"

When the rapture occurs, life on earth will be "business as usual" (*Luke 17:30*). There won't be the slightest indication it's on the horizon. Jesus said it will be "like it was in Noah's day" (*Luke 17:26*). So what was that like?

In Noah's day, people lived life normally right up until the day of the flood – even though Noah had warned them for over 100 years. His neighbors simply ignored him and went on with their lives. In fact, they staged banquets, parties, and weddings right up until the moment Noah and his family entered the ark and the flood came and destroyed the world. So Jesus is telling us that life will seem like normal right up until the very moment of the rapture.

Along similar lines, Jesus said the world before the rapture will be "as it was in the days of Lot" (*Luke 17:28*). So what were those days like? Right up until the moment Lot and his family left Sodom, the people of the city went about life as usual. It was a normal day of plowing and building, eating and drinking, and buying and selling. Then fire came from heaven and destroyed them all.

In a similar fashion, the rapture will come with no warning. Christians will be snatched away in the blink of an eye. Jesus says that as the world goes about its business, people will suddenly disappear. Two will go to bed. One will be taken, the other left. Two will be grinding flour. One will be taken, the other left (*Luke 17:31-36*).

OCCURS BEFORE THE TRIBULATION

We also know from God's character that He will not pour out His judgment on those who place their faith in Him. This is why God spared Noah and his family. It's also why God spared Lot and his family. Likewise, it would be out of character for God to pour out the judgments of the Tribulation while believers still roam the earth. Why? Because God chose to save us through

Jesus Christ, not pour His wrath upon us (*1 Thessalonians 5:9*). How can I be so sure? Because Jesus says so. He promises to keep Christians from "the great time of testing" (the Tribulation) that comes upon the whole world (*Revelation 3:10*).

In addition, we know that the restraining influence of the Holy Spirit must be taken away before the Antichrist arrives and the Tribulation takes place (*2 Thessalonians 2:5-8*). But how can the Holy Spirit be taken away? After all, the Holy Spirit resides in the hearts of all men and women who believe and trust in Jesus Christ. The only way it can be removed is if those same believers are taken away. So what does this tell us? It tells us the rapture must occur before the Tribulation.

In the end, this is all we can really know about the timing of the rapture – that it occurs before the Tribulation. After all, the rapture is a sign-less event, and once the Tribulation occurs, the world will have plenty of signs.

But the Second Coming? That's a completely different story. Why do I say that? Because the signs will tip us off. That's right. The signs. The Bible says specific signs will precede the Second Coming of Jesus Christ, and we're not only told to be familiar with them – we're commanded to look for them.

THE TIMING OF THE SECOND COMING

By its nature, the Second Coming is not an unexpected event. Because the Bible tells us it will occur at the end of the Tribulation – an event chronicled in great detail by both Daniel and John. If you read the Book of Daniel and the Book of Revelation, you'll see why that day can't sneak up on anyone like a thief in the night.

During the Tribulation, horrible judgments will rain down on the earth, more than half of the world's population will die, and the entire world will be dominated by the Antichrist. How could any of these things happen (much less all of them) and the world remain in the dark about His Coming? They can't, and that's why those who know and understand God's Word will be able to predict the timing of the Second Coming in advance.

According to Jesus, the Second Coming is an event that *must* be preceded by signs. He says there will be signs in the sun, moon, and stars (*Luke 21:25*), and there will be greater anguish on earth than at any time in history (*Matthew 24:21*). False messiahs and false prophets will perform deceptive miracles so convincing that, if possible, they could even deceive God's chosen ones (*Matthew 24:24*). How could these types of signs be present and the Second Coming of Jesus arrive "unexpectedly"? They can't.

To illustrate, here's a short (but not comprehensive) list of events that must take place before the Second Coming can occur:

- An alliance of nations led by Russia and Iran will invade Israel (*Ezekiel 38-39*)
- The Antichrist will be revealed (*2 Thessalonians 2:8*)
- Israel will sign a treaty with the Antichrist (*Daniel 9:27*)
- The Antichrist will desecrate the Temple (*Matthew 24:15*)
- The Antichrist will perform counterfeit miracles and deceive the people of the world (*2 Thessalonians 2:9-12*)
- A global government will rule the world (*Revelation 13:7*)
- Two of God's witnesses will be killed in the streets of Jerusalem and the whole world will view their bodies (*Revelation 11:1-12*)
- The armies of the world will gather together at Armageddon (*Revelation 16:16*)

How could Jesus return unexpectedly if all these events must happen first?

The reality is that Jesus *can't* return unexpectedly under such conditions. When these events finally occur, anyone familiar with the Bible will know what's coming next. Jesus verified this when He said "just as circling vultures indicate a nearby carcass, so these signs indicate the end is coming" (*Matthew 24:28*).

So if someone asks you if we can know the timing of the Second Coming, your answer should be a clear and definitive "yes." We can't know the day or the hour (*Mark 13:32*). But we can know the general timeframe.

Why? Because the Second Coming is preceded by signs – the tribulation, the antichrist, horrible judgments, and other major events.

PETER'S PROPHECY

So what's the purpose of this book? Its purpose is more than to help you understand the signs of the Second Coming. Its purpose is to point out that those signs are all around you *right now*.

Yet despite the fact these signs are all around us, people continue to mock and ridicule those who believe the Second Coming is near. Believe it or not, the apostle Peter foresaw this, and he pointed to it as a specific sign of the end.

Almost 2,000 years ago, he warned us that in the last days, people would mock the idea of Christ's return. With a sarcastic tone, he claimed they'll say exactly what we hear today – things like, "*I thought Jesus was coming back? What happened to His promise? Yet, since the beginning of the world, everything has remained the same!*" (**2 Peter 3:3-4**).

I don't know about you, but I hear people say this (or something similar to this) on a regular basis. It's accepted as fact. But is it true? Is the world "the same as it's always been"? Of course not! But that doesn't stop people from saying it is.

The truth is that the world we live in today is dramatically different from anything past generations would even remotely recognize. By itself, this isn't such a big deal. But for thousands of years the world *was* very much "the same." Don't you find that a bit strange? I do.

Keep in mind that the signs surrounding us now *weren't* present for the first 1,900+ years of Christianity, so it's not as if they've always been around. For the first time in history, Christians can point to visible signs of the imminent fulfillment of the Bible's Second Coming prophecies. Could the Millerites say the same? No. These signs weren't present for the Millerites in 1844, and they weren't present in the year 1000 or the year 1500.

But they *are* present today. Nevertheless, Peter's scoffers would have us believe that "the world is the same now as it's always been." But you'll soon see that line of thinking is absolute foolishness. In the process, I hope you'll draw the same conclusion I have – that now is the season of Christ's long-awaited return.

Now when I say this, I want to be clear. I'm not a prophet. I don't have any special knowledge from God apart from what I've read in the Bible. Jesus Himself says that "no man can know the day or the hour" of His return, and that definitely includes me. I don't know if Jesus will come next year or the year after or in 5 years, 10 years, 25 years, or 50 years. But I do know we're extremely close – within my expected lifetime for sure. Why do I say that? Because I recognize the signs.

RECOGNIZING THE SIGNS

When the disciples asked Jesus, "What will be the signs of your coming and the end of the age," He gave a detailed description of what to look for, and said "these signs indicate that the end is near" (*Matthew 24:3-28*). The signs Jesus said to look for are clear and unambiguous. They aren't hidden.

And Jesus said when you see them, you should look up because "your salvation is near" (*Luke 21:28*). In other words, when you see the signs Jesus described, you should expect His return soon.

How soon? Jesus says soon enough that the generation witnessing these signs will not pass away before His return (*Matthew 24:34*).

Did you catch that? Jesus didn't say these signs will appear and then He might come. He didn't say these signs will appear and then He'll come a thousand years later. No. He was clear. He said "this generation will not pass away" before He returns.

When He first came, Jesus rebuked the Pharisees and Sadducees for their failure to recognize the signs of the times (*Matthew 16:1-3*). Why? Because the Old Testament prophets foretold His Coming. In fact, the prophet Daniel foretold the *exact year* of His arrival! And the prophets revealed intimate details about the Messiah's birth, ministry, miracles, and ultimate death and resurrection.

Jesus scolded these religious leaders saying, "You know how to predict the weather by looking at the sky, but you don't know how to interpret the signs of the times!" The Pharisees and Sadducees knew these prophecies better than anyone else, but they chose to ignore them.

In the same way, Jesus will hold us accountable for our failure to recognize the signs of His Second Coming. You see, He wasn't just talking to the Pharisees and the Sadducees. He was talking to you and me.

Think about it. If you see a pregnant woman, it's a safe bet she'll give birth to a baby soon. You may not know what day or hour she'll give birth. But you know it's coming. And when you see dark clouds on the horizon, what do you think? A storm is coming, right?

Well, Jesus says if you can identify those events from the signs you see ahead of time, you can also identify the general time of His arrival based on the signs you see. And He clearly tells us what those signs are. He also says when you see them, His return will quickly follow. You may not know the year, the day, or the hour. But you're expected to identify the season – just like you would identify a storm cloud on the horizon.

So let's take a look at some of the signs the Bible tells us to look for. I'm certain that if you study these signs, you'll recognize them all around you. And what will you conclude? Perhaps the same thing I have – that Jesus is right at the door. That He's coming, and **now** is the season of His return.

CHAPTER 3
SIGN #1: THE EXPONENTIAL CURVE

F OR CENTURIES, HINDU pilgrims have traveled to a little village in India named Ambalappuzha to visit the Sri Krishna temple. While there, they receive a food called paal payasam free-of-charge. Why they receive this food is explained in a fable as old as India itself. It's called the Legend of Paal Payasam.

As the legend goes, one day the Hindu god Krishna appeared to the king disguised as an old sage. Knowing how much the king loved to play chess, the old sage challenged him to a friendly game. The king agreed and told the sage he could choose anything in the kingdom as his prize if he won.

As a man of humble means, the old sage asked for just a small bit of rice. However, he requested the rice be paid out in an unusual way. For each square on the chess board, he wanted the rice delivered in this manner... One grain of rice on the first square, two grains of rice on the second, four grains on the third, and so on and so on – with the amount of rice doubling for each square on the board.

The king felt bad. Surely the old sage wanted something more than this? But despite the king's encouragement to choose something more, the sage insisted he was content with the promised reward, so the two moved forward with their game.

Before long, the king acknowledged his defeat and ordered one of his attendants to fetch a bag of rice and pay the old sage. So the king's servant opened a bag of rice and started to count out the grains – one grain, two grains, four grains, eight, sixteen, thirty-two, etc. But the king soon realized the enormity of his wager. A chess board has sixty-four squares, and the payout on square twenty alone was over a million grains of rice! By square thirty – a billion! In total, the final payout would be more than *18 quintillion* grains of rice – more than all the rice in India!

When the king realized he would not be able to pay off his wager, his opponent finally revealed himself as Krishna. He told the king he could pay off the debt over time by providing free paal payasam (which is made of rice) free-of-charge to the pilgrims who enter the temple each day.

Clever, huh? Maybe you've heard that fable before. Or at least one like it. I've heard versions where the rice is wheat or where the old sage is the inventor of chess or where the game isn't chess at all, but checkers. I'm sure there are dozens upon dozens of variations of this story. But it doesn't really matter. What matters is the lesson.

THE POWER OF EXPONENTIAL GROWTH

If you plotted a graph of the grains of rice the king had to pay out on each square, you would quickly see why he made such a foolish bet. Early on, the number of rice grains appears to be insignificant. The early doubling from one to two and two to four and four to eight – doesn't, at first glance, fully reveal what's happening. It's not until you start doubling larger numbers like a million and billion that most people catch on.

This is the true power of exponential growth – what looks like slow initial growth followed by a rapid increase. It's the same power behind both the growth of bacteria and compound interest alike. It's been said that Albert Einstein once said, "The most powerful force in the universe is compound interest." Of course, by all accounts, he didn't actually say that. But it's believable that he did, right? Why? Because most people intuitively grasp the power of exponential growth, and it seems logical to consider it one of the most powerful forces in the universe.

That said, what does any of this have to do with the Second Coming of Jesus? Only this… If we take the time to study history, we'll find that someone far more prominent than Albert Einstein called attention to the awe-inspiring power of exponential growth. In fact, He said it would be a major sign marking the end of the age and the Second Coming. So who was this distinguished person?

That person was Jesus Himself.

Almost 2,000 years ago, the disciples asked Him point blank, "What will be the signs of your return and the end of the age?" Jesus responded by mentioning a variety of global signs – spiritual, natural, societal, and political. And He said these signs would appear in a distinct pattern – like birth pains (*Matthew 24:3-8*).

But what did Jesus mean by the phrase "birth pains"? What could spiritual, natural, societal, and political signs possibly have in common with birth pains? Only this – birth pains, or labor contractions, are sharp pains which increase in both intensity and frequency in the moments leading up to birth. Did you catch that? They become more frequent and have greater strength leading up to the big moment, and Jesus is telling us this same pattern will precede His coming.

So what is this pattern? It's essentially an exponential curve (Exhibit A). If you were to plot labor contractions on a graph, the result would be an exponential curve that increases right up until the time the baby is born. So what Jesus is saying is that the signs He describes and the general nature of things in this world will increase in both frequency and intensity just prior to His arrival. In

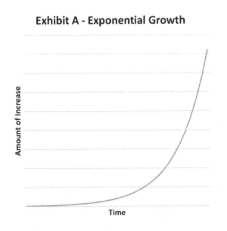

Exhibit A - Exponential Growth

other words, the signs of His Coming will increase exponentially, and this is how we'll know He's near.

General Signs

So what are these signs? And are they increasing exponentially? Many of the signs Jesus described to His disciples are general in nature, meaning they've occurred throughout history – things such as false messiahs, earthquakes, famines, and war (*Matthew 24:4-7*). But these signs have always been a part of life on earth. So many people wonder, how can these be true signs or markers of the end times if these are common events that have taken place throughout history?

The answer is clear. It's not the signs themselves, but the unprecedented method in which they'll appear. By saying these events will be the beginning of birth pains, Jesus is saying that they will increase exponentially prior to His return. Wars will kill more and more people. High magnitude earthquakes will occur with greater frequency. And famines and the other signs He describes will impact more people more frequently as the end nears.

So do we see any evidence of these signs increasing exponentially in our world today? Yes. In fact, the evidence is all around us.

Weapons and Wars

Think about it. For most of human history, wars were fought primarily in one way – through individual hand-to-hand combat. You had a spear, a sword or a club. And the other guy had his. You didn't kill someone from a hundred yards away, you did it up close and personal. And for the most part, you killed your enemies one-at-a-time. This way of fighting ruled the world for thousands of years – from Cain and Abel down through the ages.

Sure, there were advancements in warfare. But these advancements were part of a steady, seemingly incremental progression toward more powerful and deadly weapons. Cain and other early people most likely used their hands or crude weapons like tree branches and rocks as weapons. But it didn't take long for people to fashion custom weapons like flint arrowheads, knives, and spears. The Bronze Age quickly followed. By combining

copper and tin at high temperatures, people created swords, daggers, and axes significantly stronger than copper or polished rock. Then came the Iron Age. Iron sharpened easier, and when added to carbon, it produced superior steel weapons – far less likely to break or fracture than stone or bronze.

Then the Chinese developed gunpowder. When knowledge of gunpowder made its way to Europe, the Europeans invented more accurate firearms, eventually using them to conquer the New World. The Stone Age weapons of the indigenous people proved no match for gunpowder.

Throughout this whole process, it took thousands of years for man to make the relatively small advance from clubs and sticks to the development of accurate firearms. Yet, throughout all these advancements in weaponry, hand-to-hand combat remained the dominant method of war. In other words, since the dawn of time, "things were much the same as they had always been."

But since the dawn of the 20th Century, it's a different story. The outbreak of World War I in 1914 revealed the development of airplanes and balloons which could drop large explosives from the sky, the design of armored vehicles that could advance over waves of oncoming soldiers, the introduction of weapons of mass destruction such as poison gas that could kill large numbers of people indiscriminately, and the power of rapid fire machine guns that would allow a single person to fire more small-caliber rounds in one minute than 80 men equipped with rifles.

Twenty-five years later, World War II revealed the development of even more powerful weapons, including the nuclear bomb – a single weapon capable of destroying an entire city in the blink of an eye. Weapons couldn't possibly advance beyond that, right?

Yet, in the decades since, the introduction of jet airplanes, hydrogen bombs, nuclear armed submarines, and even weapons in space have revolutionized warfare.

Today, we have unmanned drones capable of dropping precision bombs that can fly right through the front door of a terrorist hideout. We have robotic spies the size of mosquitoes, and defense systems capable of destroying an incoming missile in mid-air. And the destructive power of our weapons? Even Syria, the 54th most populous nation on earth, is suspected of having a stockpile of chemical and biological weapons large enough to kill the entire population of the earth twelve times over. Just a single drop (100mg) of Sarin gas will kill the average person in a few minutes, and some experts speculate that Syria has more than 100 tons of Sarin gas, enough to kill more than 90 billion people if effectively delivered.

But so far, nothing has promised more destruction than the development of nuclear weapons. The bombs dropped on Hiroshima and Nagasaki in World War II unleashed the equivalent energy of approximately 20,000 tons of TNT. Nevertheless, just 16 years later, the Soviet Union tested the most powerful nuclear weapon ever, a hydrogen bomb nicknamed the Tsar Bomba. It unleashed the equivalent power of 50 million tons of TNT – *more than 2,500 times* as much explosive power as the bombs dropped on Hiroshima and Nagasaki!

Clearly, the destructive capacity of our weapons and war-making ability has increased exponentially. After thousands of years of small, seemingly incremental advancements in weapons technology, we've experienced a sudden and rapid increase in innovation. And this innovation shows no signs of slowing down. In just 150 years, we've gone from generals on horseback to generals in computer command and control centers.

Given the increased destructive power of our weapons, it's not surprising that the slaughter of war has also increased exponentially. While estimates vary, most experts believe somewhere between 230 and 240 million people were killed by war in the 20th Century alone – that's more than the entire world population in the 1st Century! Part of this is attributable to the overall growth in world population, but it's also a result of the increased destructive power of man-made weapons of war.

If you plotted the destructive power of the world's weapons on a graph, guess what kind of curve you would get? And if you plotted the number of people killed in each century by war, guess what it would look like? If you said, "an exponential curve," you would be right.

FAMINES

As the population of the world has grown, famines have caused more and more death and destruction in their wake. In fact, while the Roman Empire's entire population at the time of Jesus is estimated to have been approximately 55 million people, the first half of the 20th Century alone witnessed these famines*:

The 1921 famine in Russia (over 5 million dead)

The 1928-1929 famine in China (over 3 million dead)

The 1932-1933 famine in Ukraine (over 7 million dead)

The 1932-1933 famine in Kazakhstan (over 1 million dead)

The 1936 famine in China (over 5 million dead)

The 1942-1943 famine in China (over 1 million dead)

The 1943 famine in Bengal, India (over 2 million dead)

The 1946-1947 famine in the Soviet Union (over 1 million dead)

The 1959-1961 famine in China (over 36 million dead)

These are approximate statistics. Numbers may vary slightly based on the referenced source.

That's more than 61 million people who perished from famine in just 40 years! Does this sound like business as usual? Are things the same today as they've always been? Of course not. The world has seen a dramatic increase in both the frequency and intensity of famines since Jesus first answered His disciples' questions.

EARTHQUAKES

How do we measure an increase in the frequency and intensity of earthquakes? After all, advanced instrumentation to detect and measure earthquakes is relatively new. The Richter Scale didn't even exist until 1935, and most seismographs at the time failed to detect and locate any earthquakes under a magnitude of about 3.0. Yet today's sensitive instrumentation routinely measures earthquakes with negative magnitudes.

So any attempt to catalogue the total number of earthquakes over any meaningful time period is reliant on distorted data. Such data will of course show an increase in the number of earthquakes in recent times, but this is attributable to advancements in seismograph technology that have enabled us to detect previously undetectable earthquakes. It's not necessarily because there's been an increase in seismic activity.

But what if we just look at modern data from the last one hundred years and look only at earthquakes that register a magnitude of 8.0 or greater? This will give us a much more accurate picture because most instrumentation during that time period was advanced enough to detect an earthquake of such enormity. And what we're trying to do is see if there's been an increase in frequency (number) and intensity (magnitude) of earthquakes. What does *that* data set show?

According to the Advanced National Seismic System (ANSS) composite catalog[1], there has been a marked increase recently in the number of earthquakes with a magnitude of 8.0 or greater:

1900's — 3 earthquakes
1910's — 0 earthquakes
1920's — 1 earthquake
1930's — 1 earthquake
1940's — 1 earthquake
1950's — 1 earthquake
1960's — 3 earthquakes
1970's — 2 earthquakes
1980's — 3 earthquakes
1990's — 7 earthquakes
2000's — 13 earthquakes
2010's — 7 earthquakes so far

[1] Advanced National Seismic System (ANSS) Composite Earthquake Catalog
http://www.ncedc.org/anss/

The 20th Century witnessed 22 earthquakes with a magnitude of 8.0 or greater, but already the 21st Century has seen 20 such earthquakes. If that pace were to continue, we would see 142 earthquakes of 8.0 magnitude or greater by the end of this century! This is one of the signs Jesus said would increase exponentially just before His arrival, and we see it happening.

World Population Growth

Another exponential trend we're witness to is the global population explosion. According to the U.S. Census Bureau[2], the figures below are estimates of the historical world population (give or take a year).

A.D. 1 – 170 million
A.D. 1804 – 1 billion
A.D. 1927 – 2 billion
A.D. 1959 – 3 billion
A.D. 1974 – 4 billion
A.D. 1987 – 5 billion
A.D. 1999 – 6 billion
A.D. 2011 – 7 billion

During the ministry of Jesus, the total world population wasn't even 200 million. Following the crucifixion, it took almost 1,800 years for the world population to reach 1 billion people. But the second billion? It came just 123 years later. The third billion? 32 years. Each billion after that? 15 years. 13 years. 12 years. 12 years. Plot these values on a graph and guess what kind of curve you'll get?

And it's not just the number of people on earth experiencing exponential growth. People are living longer than ever. It took thousands of years for the average life expectancy to consistently stay above 40 years of age. But in the past 150 years, we've seen this metric increase exponentially.

[2] U.S. Census Bureau, "Historical Estimates of World Population"
http://www.census.gov/population/international/data/worldpop/table_history.php

In 1900, average life expectancy was around 45 years. By 1950, it was 65. And today, it's close to 80. After staying relatively constant for thousands of years, the average life expectancy has doubled in the past century and a half!

This is evidenced by U.S. Social Security Administration statistics[3] showing the number of Americans age 65 and older over the past 13 decades:

1880 – 1.7 million
1890 – 2.4 million
1900 – 3.0 million
1910 – 3.9 million
1920 – 4.9 million
1930 – 6.7 million
1940 – 9.0 million
1950 – 12.7 million
1960 – 17.2 million
1970 – 20.9 million
1980 – 26.1 million
1990 – 31.9 million
2000 – 34.9 million

What explains this increase? For the most part, it's the result of plummeting infant mortality rates – which itself is the result of better healthcare procedures, the development of vaccines and medicines, increased knowledge of nutrition and disease prevention, and access to clean water. Not surprisingly, our knowledge in these areas is growing exponentially as well.

Technological Advancement

One area where things are clearly not "the same as they've always been" is technology. The rapid pace of technological change over the past century

[3] Social Security Administration, "Life Expectancy for Social Security"
"Table 2: Americans Age 65 or Older 1880-2000" http://www.ssa.gov/history/lifeexpect.html

has been nothing short of staggering. Even over the course of just a decade, the leap forward is astonishing.

For example, in 1996, I bought my first personal computer. It had a 1 GB hard drive and a total cost of $2,600. In 2006, I walked into a local warehouse retailer and spotted a display of iPods for sale. Each of these palm size devices had 30 GB of storage and a $249 price tag. That's a thirty-fold increase in storage for a tenth of the price in just 10 years time!

Think about the power at your disposal. Two hundred and fifty years ago, if you were European nobility and you wanted to listen to music, you had to hire musicians to play for you. If you wanted to hear something new, you had to commission someone like Mozart to compose it. And when you did, you didn't receive immediate gratification.

Today, an iPod is affordable for just about everyone in the modern world. You can store thousands of songs and have them played to perfection at a moment's notice. And if you want to hear something new or different, you can download it in a matter of seconds.

So what explains this astounding growth in technological power? All of it is best explained by Moore's Law. Formulated in 1965, it's named for Intel co-founder Gordon Moore, who observed that the number of transistors on an integrated circuit doubles every two years. This law strongly influences the processing speed, memory capacity, and digital display capabilities of modern electronics.

Take communication for example. For centuries, only a few relatively slow methods existed for communicating information over long distances. You could write down a message and have it delivered by horse, carrier pigeon, ship, or a network of flags or other signs strategically placed a certain distance apart. These were your only options until the 19th Century, and in some cases, they proved to be relatively expensive. On 24 October 1861, the first transcontinental telegraph system was established in the United States. Alexander Graham Bell patented the telephone in 1876, and the telephone has continued to evolve since, from party-lines to cordless phones to cell phones to smart phones. The 20th Century brought further revolutions in communication with the introduction of radio, television, email, and texting.

This phenomenon of human technological progress closely resembles the exponential curve of birth pains. Both the power and the pace of our technological advancement have progressed (and will continue to progress) at an exponential rate. As they do, the turmoil of this world will also increase exponentially.

LINEAR VS. EXPONENTIAL GROWTH

Unfortunately, most people are completely unaware of this exponential curve. Why? Because they're standing on it.

If you stand at any one point on an exponential curve, the points on either side of you look like incremental steps. It's only when you step back and look at the whole picture that the true nature of growth is apparent.

For example, let's say you're standing on the second square of a giant chess board just like the one described at the beginning of this chapter. You have two grains of rice. From your perspective, you can see one grain of rice in square one and four grains of rice in square three.

Like most people, you intuitively expect the immediate future to be a lot like the immediate past. So since the first three squares yielded seven grains of rice, you logically conclude the next three squares will yield seven grains of rice or maybe even eight or nine. But instead, the next three squares yield fifty-six grains of rice. That's eight times what you expected!

Likewise, most people expect the next ten years to be a lot like the last ten years. And they expect the next century to be a lot like the last century. Those people make a serious miscalculation. They fail to grasp the exponential nature of population and technology growth – even though both are clearly observable. This is why so many people can say, "Things are the same as they've always been…" and keep a straight face.

THE SAME OLD CLAIMS

For those who think the Second Coming is an ancient myth, the claim that Jesus will return soon is foolishness. Just as Peter said, the common response goes something like this, "*Jesus is coming, huh? Heard that one before. Yet the world goes on today just as it has in the past.*"

Does that sound like a good argument to you? Are things today the same as they've always been?

I think it's obvious they're not. Clearly the world is not "the same as it's always been." The 20th Century alone was a time of such dramatic change that it's unlikely anyone who lived prior to 1850 would recognize today's world. Has that dramatic change slowed? Not in the least. Our generation is inventing new technologies and lifestyles we would have considered science fiction just 30 years ago.

At this point, you might ask, "So what? What's the big deal, Britt? These things would've happened anyway. After all, it's the nature of populations and technology to increase exponentially. And your earthquake data is skewed. The sample size is too small to be statistically significant."

"Also, today's sophisticated instrumentation means we're detecting more and more earthquakes – earthquakes we didn't know about in the past. Even large 8.0 magnitude earthquakes. Just because these things are happening doesn't mean that Jesus Christ is coming back to earth."

These are all good arguments, and I agree with you. A lot of these events, most notably the growth in people and technology, were probably inevitable. But we know that with the benefit of hindsight. How many people predicted them **before** they occurred?

Remember, Jesus foretold these exponential increases almost 2,000 years ago. How many ancient prophets did? Where are His contemporaries who made the same predictions? Even in the 16th Century, with the Renaissance in full swing, how many people foresaw the exponential increases we now experience?

Yet Jesus **did**. And He said these increases would signal His return. Yet amazingly, He wasn't alone.

One other person also predicted these events, and he did so more than 600 years before Jesus. And you know what? He also said these events would signal the end of the age and the arrival of God's Messiah.

Who was this man? He was a Babylonian slave named Daniel. More than 2,600 years ago, he said two specific signs would be present at "the time of the end." And you know what?

Both those signs are present today.

CHAPTER 4
SIGN #2: TRAVEL AND KNOWLEDGE

I N THE LATE 15th Century, a young Portuguese navigator immersed himself in *The Travels of Marco Polo*, a 13th Century travel log describing the adventures of an Italian merchant in the Far East. Earlier in the century, a revolutionary invention made this possible – Gutenberg's movable type printing press.

The printing press allowed for the affordable mass production of books. And *The Travels of Marco Polo* was one of the most popular of its day. Its depictions of India, China, and the riches they held ultimately inspired the young man to search for a sea-based trade route.

By now, you've probably guessed who that man was. His name was Christopher Columbus. And in September 1492, he set sail across the Atlantic Ocean. His quest? A short-cut to the Orient.

But after many weeks at sea, Columbus and his crew landed in the Bahamas instead. In the years that followed, human knowledge increased significantly as books became widespread.

This vast increase and sharing of human knowledge led to new inventions and new technologies. And these new inventions fueled a geometric expansion of knowledge and discovery, including enormous strides in our ability to travel the globe.

Five hundred years later, the results are nothing short of astounding.

In 1952, the ocean liner *Blue Riband* crossed the Atlantic in less than four days – a voyage that took Columbus and his crew *five weeks*.

Do you think this is another example of "everything remaining the same since the beginning of the world?" Or is it a sign that we live in extraordinary times? I think the answer is obvious.

Human life over the past century and a half is dramatically different than anything that came before. The breadth of our collective knowledge and the speed at which we travel have both increased exponentially.

Was all of this unforeseen? No.

Six centuries before Jesus predicted the exponential curve of the last days, a great man of God predicted our modern day explosion in travel and knowledge.

DANIEL

Twenty-six hundred years ago, Babylon was the most powerful kingdom in the world. Its king, Nebuchadnezzar, held more power than any man on earth. But Nebuchadnezzar wasn't even the wisest man in his own kingdom. That title belonged to a Hebrew slave named Daniel.

Daniel rose to great fame and power in Babylon due to his ability to interpret one of the king's mysterious dreams (*Daniel 2*). Later, under the reign of Darius the Mede, the king threw Daniel into a den of lions. But because of his faith in God, Daniel escaped unharmed (*Daniel 6*).

During his captivity, God showed Daniel a number of visions concerning the future. In one of these visions, God revealed several events set to take place just before the Second Coming.

But an angel told Daniel to keep these prophecies a secret until a later date. When? Until the end times, "when travel and knowledge will increase" (*Daniel 12:4*). Just in case you missed that, I'll repeat it again. Until the end times, ***when travel and knowledge will increase***.

In other words, one of the signs of the Second Coming is a general worldwide increase in travel and knowledge.

Do we see this sign today? You bet.

INCREASED TRAVEL

In the days of Daniel, most people traveled less than 50 miles from where they were born. Not in the course of a year, but in the course of a *lifetime*. As a slave carried away into captivity, Daniel was the exception not the rule. And after arriving in Babylon, he spent the remainder of his years in and around the city.

In the ancient world, routine travel from one part of an empire to another was not commonplace. It was extremely rare. And sometimes these trips took months if not years.

The fastest mode of land-based transportation? A horse. Fast forward about 2,400 years to the early 19th Century. What do you think was the fastest land-based mode of transportation back then? You got it. A horse.

Need an example of how slow early 19th Century travel was? The War of 1812 offers an excellent example. The Treaty of Ghent ended the war on December 24, 1814. But do you know when the final major battle took place?

The American victory over the British at the Battle of New Orleans occurred on January 8, 1815 – fifteen days after the Treaty of Ghent. Due to the slow travel and communications of the era, it took weeks for news of the treaty to reach the United States.

See how far we've come in just two centuries? The rate of change is breathtaking.

In terms of travel, things remained mostly the same from the days of Daniel to the Battle of New Orleans. Throughout that time, the horse dominated land travel.

Then, everything changed. And the change was both swift and dramatic. The cause? The Industrial Revolution.

In the 19th Century, the Industrial Revolution gave birth to the steam locomotive. This revolutionized the speed of travel. The average horse galloped at 30 mph, but by 1900, trains routinely traveled at twice that speed.

In the early 20th Century, the horseless carriage (the car) took the world by storm. In 1908, the Ford Motor Company produced the first Model

T – a car with a top speed of 40 mph. By the 1920's, race cars topped 100 mph.

For thousands of years, the horse remained the fastest mode of land-based travel. Yet within the span of one century, trains and cars rendered the horse obsolete. And the speed and power of human travel continued to increase throughout the 20th Century and right up to our present day. Notice a pattern here? If you graphed this increase in travel speed over the course of human history, what do you think it would it look like? That's right. An exponential curve.

Jesus said the days leading up to the Second Coming would resemble an exponential curve (**Matthew 24:3-8**). And Daniel revealed that travel and knowledge would increase in the end times. So it seems reasonable to expect an exponential increase in travel and knowledge in the time just before the Second Coming.

Need an example of what such an exponential increase might look like? Try this one. For several thousand years, men dreamed of controlled flight. But for centuries, that's all it was. A dream. But in 1903, Orville and Wilbur Wright put together an airplane that flew for 12 seconds and traveled 120 feet. Impressive, right? Yet 66 years later, Neil Armstrong stepped on the moon. Do you think that qualifies as "exponential" change?

INCREASING KNOWLEDGE

About three hundred years before Jesus, the Ptolemaic dynasty in Egypt constructed a library. Known as the Ancient Library of Alexandria, many consider it to be the greatest collection of written knowledge in the ancient world. While we don't know for sure how much knowledge was housed there, some estimates say as many 500,000 papyrus scrolls. This means the library probably housed tens of thousands of original works comparable to today's books, although some of these may have been duplicates.

Two thousand years ago, this was the height of human knowledge. Today? You probably have a bigger library within a few minutes of your home.

A few years ago, Google estimated more than 129 million books are in print, and the emergence of eBooks will quickly accelerate that count. Today, you can buy an Amazon Kindle for less than a hundred dollars and hold a library larger than the Library of Alexandria in the palm of your hand.

In terms of books alone, we've seen an exponential explosion in the amount and availability of knowledge. But Daniel's predicted increase in knowledge is not limited to books.

The 20th Century witnessed an explosion of information via newspapers, magazines, radio, television, 24/7 cable networks, the Internet, and smart phones.

In 1990, there was only one website. Think about that. Think of how much the world has changed in such a short period of time. Only one website in 1990. Six years later, the Internet had more than 100,000 websites. A decade later? *One hundred million.* As of right now, estimates are around six hundred million. And that number will be out of date by the time you read this.

That's a definite exponential increase. And the number of users over that timeframe shows a similar pattern. Today, more information is added to the Internet *every day* than existed in the Ancient Library of Alexandria.

Do you think this is a sign that things are the same now as they've always been? Or do you think we're witnessing a significant increase in knowledge? I'll go with the latter.

BIBLICAL KNOWLEDGE

When Daniel revealed that "knowledge will increase" in the end times (***Daniel 12:4***), he wasn't referring to general knowledge alone. He also meant prophetic knowledge. In other words, knowledge of the Bible and the end time prophecies in his vision would also increase.

Why do I say this? Because after seeing his vision of the end times, Daniel explained that he didn't understand what it meant (***Daniel 12:8***). The angel then told him, "Go. For what I have told you is a secret until the end times" (***Daniel 12:9***).

Why couldn't Daniel understand? And why would his vision remain a secret until the time of the end? The answer to these questions can be found in the nature of Daniel's vision.

Daniel's vision of the end times revealed a dramatically different world from the one he knew. Otherwise, why would he say he couldn't understand it? Would this have been true of a vision of A.D. 500 or A.D. 1000 or even the year 1700? Probably not. But it would absolutely be true of our world today.

Think about it. If Daniel saw our world of today in his vision, how could he explain it? What would cities with skyscrapers look like to someone who lived 2,600 years ago? How about jet airplanes? Television? Or computers? If you showed a film of our everyday world to someone in the ancient world, or even someone from just 300 years ago, they would be hard pressed to make sense of it.

But today? It's not so difficult for us to imagine such things.

KNOWLEDGE WITHOUT WISDOM

While the breadth and depth of our knowledge has exploded, it's important to note that knowledge is not the same as wisdom. You can have knowledge but still lack wisdom.

For instance, have you ever met someone who was "book smart" but lacked common sense? You probably have. They're all around us. The astrophysicist who can't balance his checkbook. The counselor or therapist who's been married and divorced three times.

We've all met people who are experts in one area of life and totally lacking in other areas. That's the way the world is today, and the Bible predicted this would be the exact condition of the world before Jesus Christ returns. Paul described the people of the last days as, "Ever learning, yet never able to understand the truth" (*2 Timothy 3:7*).

Isn't this exactly what we see today? The world is drowning in a sea of advanced knowledge and scientific discovery. Yet many people continue to deny the most basic truths, such as the existence of God.

CONCLUSION

The Book of Daniel reveals that an increase in travel and knowledge will immediately precede the Second Coming (**Daniel 12:4**). And what do we see today? A vast increase in both.

For thousands of years, the horse remained the fastest mode of transportation on land while the world's most celebrated libraries contained at best a few hundred thousand papyrus scrolls. Today, jets travel faster than the speed of sound and handheld devices store hundreds of times as much information as the Library of Alexandria.

It's clear the world we live in has transformed exponentially since the days of Daniel and Jesus. Yet people still use the argument Peter said they would use almost 2,000 years ago. If you dare to suggest that Jesus is coming back, they'll mock you.

"Oh, He's coming back is He? Christians have been saying that for 2,000 years. Yet, the world goes on just the same as it ever has. What's so different now?"

You've probably heard this same argument. Maybe you've even used this argument yourself. But do you believe it? Is our modern world no different from the past 2,000 years? Of course not.

Dramatic and unprecedented change has gripped our world for at least two centuries. The world we live in today is barely recognizable to past generations.

But even if you doubt this, there's one particular sign of the Second Coming you can't ignore. In fact, it didn't exist in *any* form of fulfillment until the late 19th Century. But today? Today, it's nothing less than a modern day miracle – fulfilled bible prophecy in our own day and time. And according to the Bible, immediately after you see this sign, you can know one thing with absolute certainty – Jesus is coming.

CHAPTER 5
SIGN #3: ISRAEL

ONE DAY BEFORE the expiration of the British Mandate over Palestine (May 14, 1948), hundreds of people spilled into the streets surrounding the Tel Aviv Museum. Inside stood a podium flanked by two banners bearing the Star of David, and in between those banners hung a picture of Theodor Herzl, founder of the modern Zionist movement. What made the museum so popular that day? The overflow crowd came to hear a man named David Ben-Gurion.

When he spoke, Ben-Gurion read the Israeli Declaration of Independence, a document officially declaring the establishment of a Jewish state named Israel. That same day, the United States recognized this declaration, and the nation of Israel came back into existence for the first time in nearly 2,000 years.

Ben-Gurion went on to become Israel's first Prime Minister. The banners that flanked him became the official flag of the new nation. And the Tel Aviv Museum? It was renamed Independence Hall.

To the world, May 14th, 1948 is just another notable date from the 20th Century. Conduct a poll of modern historians, and I'll wager that most of them will rank the Great Depression, the two World Wars, the Cold War, and numerous other 20th Century events as much more significant. Few, if any, will mention the rebirth of Israel.

But in my mind, the restoration of Israel as a nation is more than a footnote in history. And it's not just one of the most significant events of the 20th Century. It's one of the most significant events in *all of history*.

Why do I say that? Because thousands of years before it happened, the God of Abraham, Isaac, and Jacob declared it. Israel is literally fulfilled bible prophecy in our time. But it's more than that. Much more.

Why do I say that? Because Jesus said the generation that witnesses the restoration of Israel will also witness the Second Coming.

THE MIRACLE OF ISRAEL

Anyone who says God doesn't perform miracles anymore simply hasn't been paying attention. Why do I say that? Because the modern state of Israel is a miracle in our own time.

Less than four decades after the crucifixion, the Romans put down the final Jewish insurrection in Jerusalem, destroyed the Temple, and carted their conquered Jewish slaves to the farthest corners of a vast empire. The Romans renamed the area Palestine and considered the nation of Israel dead forever. Century after century passed. And the Jewish people continued to live in exile, scattered among the nations of the world.

But in the late 19th Century, something changed. A new movement called Zionism prompted thousands of Jews to immigrate to the land of their ancestors. It started with a trickle. A few thousand here. A few thousand there. Then tens of thousands. Then Hitler's Holocaust, and a trickle turned into a torrent. After the horror of the Nazi death camps, many Jews viewed the creation of a Jewish state as a basic matter of survival. The result? The Israeli Declaration of Independence and the creation of modern day Israel.

Despite the mighty Roman Empire's best efforts, despite centuries of rampant Anti-Semitic persecution, despite Stalin and Hitler – the Jewish people miraculously retained their distinct religious, racial and cultural identity *for centuries* while living as exiles among the nations of the world. And today, the nation of Israel stands again.

But how?

Why do the Jewish people thrive to this day, while other conquered ancient people assimilated among the nations? Where are the Hittites, Ammonites, Edomites, Jebosites, and Philistines? In my mind, there's only one explanation.

The Jewish people are still around for one reason and one reason only – because the God of Israel made a promise. God promised Abraham his descendants would number more than the stars in the sky (*Genesis 15:5*). The same Creator promised Solomon He would never abandon the people of Israel (*1 Kings 6:13*). And guess what? He made another promise through His prophets.

Over and over again, God promised to bring His people out of their long exile and back into the land of Israel. And that's exactly what He did.

GOD'S PROMISED RESTORATION

Throughout the Old Testament, God promised to return His people home to Israel following a long, worldwide exile. For example, in the Book of Isaiah, God promised to bring the Jewish exiles back into the land of Israel from east and west and north and south – from the farthest corners of the Earth. He also promised the Jewish people would survive and thrive despite the hardships they faced (*Isaiah 43:1-13*).

Is Isaiah 43 an isolated case? No. The Bible makes this same claim countless times. Thousands of years ago, God promised to call His people:

- from "among the nations" (*Ezekiel 39:28*)
- from "the farthest corners of the earth" (*Isaiah 11:12*), and
- from "north, south, east, and west" (*Psalm 107:3*)

And this is exactly what He did. Every single one of us is an eyewitness to the modern miracle of Israel.

Almost everyone knows the story of how God used Moses to deliver the Jewish people from Egyptian bondage. But thousands of years ago, the Bible predicted that a day will come when people no longer refer to the God of Israel as the one who rescued His people from the land of Egypt.

Instead, they will refer to Him as the one who brought His people back into the land of Israel from **all the countries in the world** where He had exiled them (*Jeremiah 16:14-15*).

Throughout the Old Testament, God made this promise. He promised to bring His people home and display His holiness to the nations (*Ezekiel 20:41-42*). He promised to bring "the remnant of His flock" back into the land of Israel from the countries where He had driven them (*Jeremiah 23:3*). He promised to welcome them home from the lands where they were scattered (*Ezekiel 20:34*). He promised to restore them to the land of Israel from distant lands (*Jeremiah 30:2, 10*). And God promised, though scattered among the nations, His people would never forget Him, and He would bring them back into the land of Israel (*Zechariah 10:9*).

This is a promise God made as early as the days of Moses:

"Then the Lord your God will restore your fortunes. He will have mercy on you and gather you back from all the nations where he has scattered you. Even though you are banished to the ends of the earth, the Lord your God will gather you from there and bring you back again. The Lord your God will return you to the land that belonged to your ancestors, and you will possess that land again." **Deuteronomy 30:3-5** *(NLT)*

God kept His promise, and His proof is the modern nation of Israel.

How God Will Restore Israel

Not only did God promise to bring His people from among the nations and back into the land, but He also told us the specific ways in which He would do so. For example, God promised that Israel would blossom agriculturally and fill the whole world with its fruit (*Isaiah 27:6*).

Did that happen? Yes. Today, the tiny nation of Israel (a desert wasteland less than a century ago) is one of the world's leading fresh citrus producers and a net exporter of more than forty varieties of fruit. God repeated this promise through the prophet Ezekiel, saying His people would re-enter the land, produce much fruit, and be more prosperous than before (*Ezekiel 36:8-11*).

More than 2,500 years before it happened, the prophet Isaiah predicted God would bring forth the nation of Israel in a single day. He likened it to a woman "who gives birth in an instant without labor pains" (*Isaiah 66:7-9*).

Did this happen? Yes. When David Ben-Gurion read the Israeli Declaration of Independence on May 14, 1948, the United States formally recognized the new Jewish state *that same day*! A new nation had come into existence in a single day – just as Isaiah foretold.

Twice, the Bible predicted that when God's people returned, Israel and Judah would no longer be rivals. Through the prophet Isaiah, He said the two would be united (*Isaiah 11:13*) – just as we see today with the modern state of Israel. God repeated this proclamation through the prophet Ezekiel, stating that the new nation would be one kingdom, no longer divided (*Ezekiel 37:22*).

THE ODDS OF SUCH A THING

What are the odds that the people of a conquered nation would be scattered among the nations of the world, yet retain their distinct racial, cultural, and religious identity in the face of unprecedented persecution for almost 2,000 years? Probably not good, right? Yet, that's the history of the Jewish people, and God foretold it through the Old Testament prophets.

In fact, God says the existence of the Jewish people in the land of Israel is evidence that He is the only God. He throws down a challenge to the unbelievers of this world – can their idols foretell such things? Can any of them predict what will happen tomorrow? (*Isaiah 41:8-24*).

They can't. But the God of Israel can!

He foretold the exile of His people centuries in advance, and likewise, He proclaimed their return.

Well, you might think, that's great. God promised to bring His people back into the land of Israel, and He did. But so what? What's the big deal? How is that a sign of the Second Coming?

It's a sign because other prophecies (prophecies yet to be fulfilled) are intimately connected with God's promise to bring His people back into the land. In fact, the prophets are clear about God's plan and what He has in store. Ezekiel 37 is a good example. It reveals that something monumental will happen soon after the return of God's people to the land of Israel.

What is this monumental event? *The Messiah will arrive to set up His everlasting kingdom* (**Ezekiel 37:24-28**).

THE TIMING OF ISRAEL'S RESTORATION

Through the prophet Hosea, God said the people of Israel will go a long time without a king, sacrifices, sacred pillars, or priests, then they will return to the land and seek their God and Messiah "in the last days" (**Hosea 3:4-5**).

Did you catch that? Did you notice when God says they will return to the land?

In the last days.

This is an Old Testament reference to the end times and the seven year period of the Tribulation.

Through the prophet Joel, God promised to gather the armies of the world in the Valley of Jehoshaphat. When?

At the time when God restores Judah and Jerusalem, bringing His people back from among the nations where they were scattered (**Joel 3:1-2**). In other words, God will gather the armies of the world in the Valley of Jehoshaphat in our day and time, because we're witnesses to the restored nation of Israel.

So what is the Valley of Jehoshaphat? It's literally translated as "the valley where Yahweh judges." And it references the future gathering of the world's armies at a place most people are familiar with – Armageddon. In other words, not long after the restoration of Israel, the battle of Armageddon will take place and God will judge the world.

Need more?

Through Isaiah, God promised the desert will bloom (**Isaiah 35:1**).

This is the same promise made in *Isaiah 27:6*, and it occurs when God's people are restored to the land. Then in successive verses we learn that the blooming of the desert will be followed by *the Lord returning to destroy Israel's enemies* (*Isaiah 35:2-4*).

Through Jeremiah, God promised to gather the remnant of His flock from the nations where he had driven them and bring them back into the land (*Jeremiah 23:3-4*). Then, God promised to raise up a righteous descendant of King David, a king who will rule the land with wisdom (*Jeremiah 23:5-6*).

Who is this righteous King? The long-awaited Messiah.

And when will He come to rule? *When the people are back in the land* (*Jeremiah 23:7-8*).

Through Micah, God promised to gather His exiles and form them into a strong nation. Then, He promised to rule from Jerusalem as their king forever (*Micah 4:6-7*). How long? *Forever.*

This promise to restore Israel immediately follows a Messianic passage describing the Millennial Kingdom of Jesus Christ. It's the same chapter with the famous verse, "They shall beat their swords into plowshares and their spears into pruning hooks, and nation will not fight nation, nor will there be war anymore" (*Micah 4:3*). This is a radically different world where no one lives in fear, a world of unprecedented peace and prosperity where God rules the nations. And God clearly states that this time period will follow the restoration of His people in the land of Israel.

Convinced? If not, that's okay. Because we're just getting started. The Book of Isaiah reveals even more evidence regarding the timing of Israel's restoration.

ISRAEL'S RESTORATION ACCORDING TO ISAIAH

Over and over again, the prophet Isaiah relayed God's promise to bring back the exiled people of Israel and form a new nation. But one chapter in Isaiah is of particular interest – Chapter 11.

In it, not only does God promise to restore the nation of Israel and raise its flag among the nations (*Isaiah 11:12*), but He makes additional promises as well.

What are these promises? That the wolf and the lamb will lie together. That leopards will lie down with goats. That even a baby can play with a cobra and not be bitten! (*Isaiah 11:6-9*).

Why? Because the heir to David's throne (Jesus Christ) will rule over the nations, transforming the world into a place of peace and tranquility (*Isaiah 11:10*).

And when does God say this will happen? You got it. After His people are re-gathered from distant lands and the ends of the earth (*Isaiah 11:11-12*) and after Israel is reborn as a single, unified nation (*Isaiah 11:13*).

In other words, the restoration of Israel as a nation will immediately precede the Millennial Kingdom of Jesus Christ. Shortly after its rebirth, Jesus will return to earth and rule from Jerusalem!

At this point, you might say, *"Now wait a minute, Britt. Maybe you're right, but John said we were in the last hour nearly 2,000 years ago (1 John 2:18). The Second Coming may well occur after the Jews return to Israel, but it might be a 1,000 years after they return. What makes you so sure He's coming in our lifetime?"*

What makes me so sure is this – Jesus said so. Remember, Jesus said to look for certain signs, and when you see them, He said to look up and get ready for His return. So a long interval of time between the appearance of these signs and His Coming just wouldn't make sense. It would be misleading at best, and Jesus isn't in the business of misleading people. But fortunately, we don't have to speculate. Because Jesus flat out told us the restoration of Israel will immediately precede His return.

JESUS AND THE FIG TREE

Throughout the Old Testament, the fig tree is often used as a symbol for the nation of Israel. For example, God compared the people of Israel to ripe figs (*Hosea 9:10*). He also compared the Babylonian exiles to good figs (*Jeremiah 24:5-7*).

In a similar way, Jesus used the fig tree as a symbol for Israel. Need an example? In one of His parables, Jesus taught about a man who planted a fig tree in his garden. Day after day, he came to the tree to see if there was any fruit on it. But he was always disappointed.

Finally, the man told his gardener, "It's been three years, and there hasn't been a single fig! Cut it down. We can use the space for something else."

But the gardener said, "Give it one more chance. Leave it for one more year. I'll give it plenty of attention. If we get figs next year, great. If not, cut it down" (*Luke 13:6-9*).

So what's the meaning of this parable? Up to that time, Jesus had publicly spread His message in Israel for three years, performing miracles, exhibiting unprecedented knowledge of the Scriptures, and offering ample evidence of His claim to be the long awaited Messiah. Yet despite three years of testimony, Israel refused to believe in the one who was sent.

According to this parable, Jesus agreed to give Israel one more year to bear fruit (Jesus told this parable about a year before His crucifixion). If the fig tree (Israel) failed to bear fruit following the extra year, she would be cut down (destroyed). Of course, we know from history that this happened. Israel rejected Jesus as the Messiah, and less than forty years later in A.D. 70, Rome destroyed her.

In another example, Jesus was on His way to Jerusalem when He encountered a fig tree on the side of the road. Hungry, He searched its branches for some figs to eat, yet He found nothing but leaves. So Jesus cursed the tree, saying "May you never bear fruit again!" And immediately, the fig tree withered (*Matthew 21:18-19*).

Do you think Jesus was really upset with a fig tree? Of course not. This story has a much deeper meaning. Just like the Luke 13 parable, the fig tree and its fruit are symbols of the nation of Israel and its rejection of the Messiah.

In this case, the fig tree (Israel) failed to bear fruit (faith in Him) even though its leaves indicated it was in season (the appointed time for the coming of the Messiah). So due to its lack of fruit, the fig tree withered – indicating that Israel would soon be destroyed as a nation.

CHAPTER 5

So what's my point? Only this – Jesus said when we see the fig tree (Israel) grow leaves and sprout (regenerate), we should pay close attention. Why? Because when that happens, *He will return within a single generation.*

THE SIGN OF OUR GENERATION

When the disciples asked Jesus to reveal the "signs of His Coming and the end of the age," Jesus responded with a detailed description of signs and events that would transpire just prior to His return. But when He concluded His description, He told them **when** these things would happen.

He didn't give them a specific date or time. Instead, He told them to look for one particular sign, and when that sign appeared, they would know He was right at the door, ready to return. What was that sign?

The nation of Israel.

Speaking to His disciples, Jesus once again used the fig tree as a symbol for the nation of Israel. He said, "Just as you know that summer is near when you see the leaves sprout on the fig tree, when you see these events happen, you know the time is near" (*Matthew 24:32-33*).

Does this sound familiar? It should. Jesus used a similar analogy when speaking to the Pharisees and Sadducees. He said they could recognize the dark clouds in the sky and tell that rain was coming, but they couldn't recognize the signs of the times. In similar fashion, most people can look at blooming plants in the spring and know that summer is near.

But when Jesus is explaining the signs of His Coming and the end of the age, He isn't simply using the fig tree in bloom as an analogy of how to notice signs. He's telling them it's *the sign*.

Just as the fig tree of Israel withered and died when it failed to recognize the Messiah, the fig tree of Israel will regenerate and sprout its leaves again just prior to His Second Coming. In other words, Israel will be "in season" once again, ready to receive her Messiah.

In fact, Jesus assures us that once God's people are back in the land of Israel, we've reached the generation of His return. He says the generation witnessing the restoration of Israel as a nation will not die out before all the events He described take place (***Matthew 24:34***). And what are the events He described?

The Tribulation, His Second Coming, and the end of the age.

The reestablishment of Israel as a nation is the foremost sign to our generation that the return of Jesus is imminent. It's been six decades since Israel was once again declared a nation against all worldly odds. People who were alive when Israel became a nation are still around, but time is running short. Who knows how long we have, but it won't be hundreds of years of signs gathering momentum. It will be within a "generation" – whatever that means. Jesus is coming. The fig tree is in bloom, and we are the generation He spoke of.

Think I'm wrong? You're not alone.

Just as Peter prophesied, there's no shortage of people willing to scoff at the idea of His Return, saying "*Where's Jesus? You've been telling us He's coming. But the world goes on just as it always has.*" Yet, the world today does not "go on just as it always has." The fact that the Jewish people are back in the land of Israel is evidence enough.

God promised to bring His people back into the land, and He did. This is a major sign of the Second Coming – one of the biggest of all. For 1,878 years, Christians could not point to this sign. Now they can. Don't you find that interesting? I do.

But while the nation of Israel is an important sign, it's not the *only* sign. The Bible also said the Jewish people would reclaim a particular City. And guess what? Jesus said when that happens, the end of the age will come.

CHAPTER 6
SIGN #4: JERUSALEM

ON THE THIRD day of the Six-Day War in June of 1967, the Israeli Defense Force powered its way into the Old City of Jerusalem. Within a few hours, the Israeli Paratroop Brigade took possession of the Temple Mount, giving Israel control over its holiest site for the first time in almost nineteen centuries.

Jews celebrated in Israel and around the world. For the first time in almost two decades, they had access to and were free to worship at the Temple Mount and the Western Wall. For most of the world, it was a historic, yet unexpected and surprising event. Photographers captured the triumphant celebrations, and news outlets broadcast Israel's victory all over the world.

In my mind, it's one of the most important days in the past 2,000 years. Why? Because I know what the Bible says about the Jewish people and Jerusalem. And you know what? I'm not alone.

At the time, IDF Chief Rabbi Shlomo Goren also recognized the significance of that day. When the IDF secured the Temple Mount, he gathered in prayer with several soldiers at the Western Wall. Torah scroll in hand, he blew a Shofar (ram's horn). Then he announced, "*We have taken the city of God. We are entering the Messianic era for the Jewish people...*"

Find that interesting? I do.

After all, Goren proclaimed the beginning of the Messianic area. What in the world did he mean by that? What he meant is that he understood the significance of the moment. Rabbi Goren knew the writings of the prophets and what they say. And what do they say? They say the Messiah will come when God's people are gathered back in the land. But they also say something else. They say the Messiah will come when the Jewish people are back in the land *and* the City of Jerusalem.

Knowing what the prophets said, and knowing they have a perfect track record when it comes to fulfilled prophecy, can you see now why June 7th, 1967 was so important?

FULFILLMENT OF OLD TESTAMENT PROPHECY

When the IDF captured Jerusalem in June 1967, the whole world witnessed the fulfillment of ancient bible prophecy. Why do I say that? Because the Bible not only predicted the gathering of the Jews back in the land of Israel, it also said they would once again inhabit the City of Jerusalem. Think I'm making this up? Go grab your Bible.

More than 2,500 years ago, the prophet Zechariah said God would bring His people back from the east, west, north, and south and plant them safely in the City of Jerusalem (*Zechariah 8:7-8*). Did this happen? It did.

We saw in the last chapter that after more than eighteen centuries of exile, God brought the Jewish people from the farthest corners of the earth – from east, west, north, and south – and planted them once again in the land of Israel. On May 14, 1948, the nation of Israel reappeared on the world scene. This fulfilled God's promise as communicated through several Old Testament prophets.

But in Zechariah 8, we learn that God promised those same people would not only inhabit the land of Israel, but also the City of Jerusalem. And that's why the Six-Day War is so important. When the IDF took possession of the Temple Mount and east Jerusalem, they fulfilled Zechariah's prophecy.

Alone, this is nothing less than a miracle. But it's not an isolated event. Zechariah had much more to say.

THE WORLD'S MOST DIVISIVE CITY

All those centuries ago, Zechariah also foresaw the present day world conflict over the City of Jerusalem. Quoting God, he said, "I will make Jerusalem an intoxicating drink for all the nations who try to divide her." (*Zechariah 12:2-3*).

Do we see this today? Absolutely!

The City of Jerusalem is ground zero in the Arab-Israeli conflict. It's the epicenter of world diplomacy. Who should govern it? And how? These are the questions at the heart of the ongoing conflict between the Jews, the Arabs, and the United Nations.

In 1980, Israel named Jerusalem its undivided capital. But much of the world refuses to recognize Jerusalem as an Israeli city, much less Israel's capital.

Many in the United Nations view Jerusalem as an "international city," while the Arabs believe it should be the capital of a newly declared Palestinian state. Others believe it should be divided among various factions. But while a number of opinions exist, the majority of world opinion is dead set against Israel and its continued "occupation" of Jerusalem. And the most powerful nations in the world, including the United States, constantly pressure Israel to trade "land for peace."

Without a doubt, this is current evidence of the initial fulfillment of Zechariah's prophecy. Why do I say "initial"? Because Zechariah has much more to say about what happens once Jerusalem is in the hands of the Jews.

SO WHAT?

At this point, you might be thinking, "*Okay, Britt. I get it. The Jews are back in Jerusalem, just like they're back in the land of Israel. But so what? How is this connected to the Second Coming?*"

It's such a big deal because the Bible says the Messiah will come in triumph only when the Jews have been reestablished in their land *and* in the City of Jerusalem. That's why Rabbi Goren said, "*We are entering the Messianic era*" back in 1967.

Again, more than 2,500 years ago, the prophet Zechariah relayed God's promise to bring His people back from the east, west, north, and south and plant them safely in the City of Jerusalem (*Zechariah 8:7-8*). God promised that old men and women will gather in the city squares, while the streets of the city are filled with children at play (*Zechariah 8:4-5*). Today, we are witnesses to the fulfillment of these prophecies. The Jewish people are back in the land. They're back in the City of Jerusalem. And guess what? The elderly walk the same streets where children play.

Less than a hundred years ago, all of this seemed impossible. But you know what? It happened. Just as God promised, it happened.

And in the same chapter of Zechariah, God made another promise. Do you know what that promise was?

God promised to return to Mount Zion and live in Jerusalem (*Zechariah 8:3*). Did you catch that? God said He's coming to live in Jerusalem! And just so there's no confusion, God doesn't mean that in a symbolic or spiritual sense. He means it literally. His actual physical presence will dwell in Jerusalem. This is a reference to the Kingdom of Jesus Christ.

Zechariah says people from all over the world will travel to Jerusalem to worship the Lord and ask for His blessing. In those days, ten foreigners will grab the sleeve of one Jew and say, "Let us walk with you for we hear that God is with you" (*Zechariah 8:20-23*).

Can you believe that? What a contrast to this present age where the majority of the world despises the Jewish people and anti-Semitism is rampant!

Here, Zechariah says the gathering of the Jewish people back in the land and back in Jerusalem will usher in the Messiah's eternal Kingdom. In other words, once the Jews are back in Jerusalem, the Second Coming is close at hand.

Not convinced? Then maybe Jesus can help. Why do I say that?

Because Jesus Himself pointed to the Jewish possession of Jerusalem as a sign of His return. He told His disciples to flee for the hills when they see the sacrilegious object Daniel spoke of standing in the Temple (*Matthew 24:15-16*). Now think about that.

Before the Antichrist desecrates the Temple, it must exist. Right now, it doesn't. The Romans destroyed the Temple in A.D. 70. So for Jesus to be right, the Temple must be rebuilt. Otherwise, how could it be desecrated? And before it can be rebuilt, the Jews must control Jerusalem. As of June 7, 1967, they do.

And you want to know what else? Jesus says the Israeli possession of Jerusalem will *immediately* precede His Second Coming.

A SIGN OF HIS COMING

When visiting Herod's Temple, the disciples commented on its majesty and splendor, marveling at the beauty of its stonework. But Jesus' reaction? He told them the time would soon come when not one stone would be left on top of another (*Luke 21:5-6*).

The disciples asked when this would happen, and Jesus went on to describe the destruction of the Temple and the scattering of the Jews into all the nations (*Luke 21:24*).

In A.D. 70, the Romans besieged Jerusalem and destroyed the Temple. In burning the Temple, all its golden ritual objects melted and gold poured into the cracks between the stones. To retrieve the gold, the Romans broke apart and overturned every stone. This fulfilled the words Jesus spoke to His disciples.

In A.D. 135, the Romans put down the final Jewish insurrection, renamed Israel "Palestine," and carried her people to the farthest parts of the Roman Empire.

Then Jesus made a statement that's one of the keys to understanding the timing of His return. He told the disciples this: Jerusalem "will be trampled by the Gentiles until the times of the Gentiles come to an end," *and then He will return* (*Luke 21:24-28*).

The destruction of the Temple in A.D. 70 by Titus and the Roman legions initiated the "times of the Gentiles." For centuries thereafter, Gentile kings and kingdoms exercised control over the Temple Mount and the Old City of Jerusalem. Here's a rough timeline of control over Jerusalem:

Roman Empire (70-325)

Byzantine Empire (325-637)

The Caliphates (637-1099)

The Crusaders (1099-1187)

The Mamluks (1187-1516)

Ottoman Empire (1516-1917)

British Empire (1917-1948)

Israel/Jordan (1948-1967)

Israel (1967-Present)

From the destruction of the Temple in A.D. 70 to the Six Day War in A.D. 1967, Jerusalem was in the hands of people other than Jews. For 1,897 years, the Jews did not control Jerusalem. Today, they do. Is this just a coincidence? I don't think so.

Nearly 2,000 years ago, Jesus said this would happen. He said Jerusalem would be surrounded by armies, the Temple destroyed, and the Jews scattered in exile throughout the world. Then He said the Gentiles will trample Jerusalem "until the times of the Gentiles come to an end" (*Luke 21:20-24*). Then what?

Then Jesus says, "The entire world will see the Son of Man coming in great power and glory" (*Luke 21:27*). This is a direct reference to the "Son of Man" prophesied in the Book of Daniel (*Daniel 7:13-14*), the Messiah who will set up an everlasting kingdom of peace and righteousness. Here, Jesus is telling us point blank that when the Jews are back in Jerusalem, it's a sign that His return is just around the corner.

Knowing this, do you still buy into the idea that "things are the same now as they've always been?" After almost 2,000 years of foreign control of Jerusalem, the Old City is back in Jewish hands. Coincidence? No. The Bible foretold it, and it's only one of many signs that point to the Second Coming.

For instance, the Bible also prophesied the reaction of Israel's surrounding neighbors and the entire world community. And today, we see those prophecies fulfilled before our eyes as well.

CHAPTER 7
SIGN #5: ISRAEL'S NEIGHBORS

I N LATE 2005, Iranian President Mahmoud Ahmadinejad made world headlines. What exactly made him newsworthy? At a conference in Tehran titled "The World Without Zionism," he said he agreed with the Ayatollah Khomeini who said the "occupying regime" (Israel) must be "wiped off the map." Strong language, right? Unfortunately, it wasn't the first or the last such statement from Ahmadinejad.

At a 2008 celebration commemorating the death of Khomeini, Ahmadinejad said "the terrorist Zionist regime" will soon "disappear off the geographical scene." In countless speeches, over and over, Ahmadinejad expressed his desire to see the nation of Israel destroyed and her territory given to the Muslim people. And you know what? His view is shared among the ruling Ayatollahs, millions of Iranian citizens, and much of the Arab world.

In fact, this insatiable desire to destroy the state of Israel is as old as the nation itself. Since the Israeli Declaration of Independence on May 14, 1948, Israel and her Muslim neighbors have engaged in approximately seven conventional wars. Leader after leader among the surrounding nations has set his sights on the destruction of Israel.

In the 1950's and 1960's, Egyptian President Gamal Abdel Nassar was one of them. And he was followed by a host of others just like him. Yassar Arafat, Ayatollah Khomeini, Muammar Gaddafi, Osama Bin Laden, and countless other Muslim leaders have called for Israel's destruction. And groups like the PLO, Islamic Jihad, Hamas, Hezbollah, and the Muslim Brotherhood all share the same dream as Ahmadinejad. They literally live for the day when the nation of Israel is wiped off the map.

What they don't know is that thousands of years ago, the Old Testament prophets foresaw this deep-seated hatred for Israel. And guess what? You got it. They said it's a sign of the last days and a precursor to the Second Coming.

"GOD'S LAND BELONGS TO US"

Looking at the Middle East today, it's no surprise that the nations and people surrounding Israel share Ahmadinejad's Anti-Semitism. Why? Because the Old Testament prophets foretold their negative reaction to a restored Israel.

More than three thousand years ago, the prophet Asaph claimed the nations surrounding the restored nation of Israel would be unanimous in their contempt for Israel. He said they will say "Come, let us wipe away the nation of Israel. Let's destroy the memory of its existence" (*Psalm 83:4*) and "Let us take for ourselves these pasturelands of God" (*Psalm 83:12*).

Do those statements sound familiar? They should. They're almost word for word what we hear in the Middle East today. And we've heard these same declarations from the Muslim world over and over again since May 14, 1948.

So who exactly are the people the Bible predicts will say these things? In Psalm 83, Asaph states the following nations will conspire against the people of Israel (*Psalm 83:6-8*):

Edomites

Ishmaelites

Moabites

Hagrites

Gebalites

Ammonites

Amalekites

The people of Philistia

The people of Tyre

The people of Assyria
The descendants of Lot

So who are these people today? That's a good question. If you were to visit these geographical areas today, you would find that they're home to Israel's most noted enemies. Below are the modern day names of the geographic areas where those ancient people once resided:

Edomites – Southern Jordan
Ishmaelites – Northwestern Saudi Arabia
Moabites – Central Jordan
Hagrites – Eastern Jordan
Gebalites – North Lebanon
Ammonites – Northern Jordan
Amalekites – Southern Israel and the Gaza Strip
Philistia – The Gaza Strip
Tyre – Southern Lebanon
Assyria – Syria / Northern Iraq
Descendants of Lot – Jordan

So what are these nations doing today? The Gaza Strip is literally governed by Hamas, an Islamic terrorist organization committed to the destruction of Israel. Hamas is also highly influential in the West Bank and the nation of Jordan. And Lebanon? Much of Lebanon is home to Hezbollah, a Shiite Muslim terrorist organization committed to the destruction of Israel.

The other nations? Syria is certainly no friend of Israel, and they have a long history of harboring terrorists. Saudi Arabia? Saudi Arabia is primarily responsible for the worldwide funding of radical Wahhabist madrassas. These schools promote Islamic militancy and violent jihad against Israel and the West. In fact, the Taliban is a product of the Saudi funded madrassas in Pakistan, where Osama Bin Laden is revered.

Ezekiel predicted these same neighbors would say "God has given their land to us" (*Ezekiel 11:14-17*), and "Israel and Judah are ours. We will take possession of them. What do we care if their God is there?" (***Ezekiel 35:10***). Isn't this what we read in the headlines every day? It is.

The Muslims claim the land of Israel belongs to them, that "the mountains of Israel have been given to us" (***Ezekiel 35:12-13***). Syria, which lost the strategically important Golan Heights in the Six-Day War joins a chorus of Israeli detractors in claiming "the Golan Heights belong to us" (***Ezekiel 36:2***).

This determination to destroy Israel has resulted in repeated threats and violence. Israel has been the target of terrorist bombings, rocket attacks, and conventional wars. In fact, since its inception in May 1948, the modern state of Israel has engaged in no less than half a dozen conventional wars with her neighbors. Why? One reason and one reason only. Because Israel's neighbors claim the land belongs to them – exactly as Ezekiel foretold more than 2,600 years ago.

THE ISRAELI DEFENSE FORCE

Given just the conventional wars alone – 1948, 1956, 1967, 1973, etc. – don't you find it strange that Israel has won ***all*** of them? Keep in mind, Israel is one of the world's smallest nations. And prior to 1967, it was even smaller than it is now! Don't you find it curious that one of the world's smallest nations is also one of its greatest military powers?

Yet, God predicted this outcome too – centuries in advance. More than six hundred years before Jesus, God said the enemies of Israel will possess her land, including the Golan Heights. "But," said God. "I will bring them back" (***Ezekiel 36:1-5***).

In his Valley of the Dry Bones vision (where God breathes life back into the Jewish people), the prophet Ezekiel says the Jewish people came to life and stood up as ***an exceedingly great army***" (***Ezekiel 37:10***).

Zechariah repeated this promise, speaking of a day when Israel is like a fire among sheaves of grain, burning up the neighboring nations (***Zechariah 12:6***). In fact, he claims even the weakest soldier among them will be like David (***Zechariah 12:8***).

Remember the story of David? While still a boy, he took on the most fearsome warrior of his time, a giant named Goliath. If Las Vegas had existed three thousand years ago, the odds of David defeating Goliath would have been astronomical. Yet David won. Why? He won because God was on his side.

Notice any similarities between David and the nation of Israel today? What are the odds of Israel winning four conventional wars in a 25 year period? Israel barely cracks the Top 100 nations in terms of population, but its military consistently ranks among the most powerful in the world. The whole country is less than 13,000 square miles (approximately the size of New Jersey). That's **less than one-tenth of one percent** of the land mass of the surrounding nations that wish to destroy her. Does this sound like a recipe for "an exceedingly great army"?

Yet, that's exactly what the IDF is. Surrounded on all sides, a brand new nation that didn't even have a formal military emerged from a multi-front war as the victor in 1948. With Syria, Jordan, and Egypt preparing for war, the Israelis struck preemptively in 1967. The result? They achieved overwhelming victory *in just six days*.

Caught by surprise on Yom Kippur in 1973, her enemies almost cut Israel in half within 48 hours. But the IDF quickly won back all the territory it lost in the opening days of the war, and the world brokered a truce with the IDF at the gates of Cairo and Damascus. Against all odds, Israel always seems to come out on top.

THE ULTIMATE OUTCOME

Why is this? While many of Israel's neighbors would love to see the Jewish state destroyed, they've overlooked an important point. What have they overlooked? A promise made by God. And that promise is that Israel will stand forever.

According to the Book of Amos, God promised to bring His people back from their faraway lands of exile and firmly plant them in Israel, never to be uprooted again (*Amos 9:11-15*). Now stop for a minute.

Did you read that? If not, I'll repeat it. God said the Jews are in Israel never to be uprooted again. *Never.*

Given the impeccable track record of bible prophecy, this should be a clear message to Israel's enemies. Despite the longing of millions of Muslims to destroy her, and despite Ahmadinejad's promise to "wipe Israel off the map," God has other plans. Would you bet against Him?

I wouldn't. But tens of millions of Muslims are more than willing. They continue to pursue their dream of "pushing the Jews into the sea" with the same level of enthusiasm and determination. They aren't deterred by more than six decades of failure. They still believe Allah will come through, and throughout the world, millions of non-Muslims believe it to.

These people don't think the God of Israel exists, and God knows it. That's why He's promised to make Himself known through fulfillment of His promises to Israel. God says He will "punish those who mistreat the exiles (the Jews)" (*Ezekiel 28:25-26*), and He will execute His judgment on those around Israel who hate them (*Ezekiel 28:25-26*).

Islamic dreams of the future destruction of Israel are just that – dreams. Israel isn't going anywhere. Not only will she survive as promised, but her enemies will be the ones destroyed.

THE TIMING OF THESE EVENTS

At this point, you may be again thinking, *"Okay, Britt. Even if the Bible did predict these events, what does it have to do with the Second Coming?"*

Only this – the Bible claims Israel's neighbors will lay claim to her land and try to "wipe her off the map" at a specific time in history. And when is that time? When "the time of Israel's iniquity comes to an end" (*Ezekiel 35:5*). In other words, when God brings His people back into the land of Israel, after they've been scattered among the nations in a long exile. That's the point in time when her neighbors will be so belligerent.

And what does the Bible say about the timing of the IDF's emergence as a military power? When does it say Israel will have an "exceedingly great army"? The Bible says when God's people are re-gathered in the land just before the Messiah returns (*Ezekiel 12, 36, 37*). When the Jewish people have been "brought back from the nations where they were scattered, and given the land of Israel by God" (*Ezekiel 11:17*).

Think about it. The surrounding nations desperate to "wipe Israel off the map…" Israel as a great military power… And punishment of the nations that despise Israel… These are all things we see today. We see these events playing out in the aftermath of a restored Israel, just as the prophets foretold.

In the Book of Ezekiel, God promised to reveal Himself to the nations. First, by gathering His people from among the nations where He scattered them. Second, by punishing the surrounding nations that spew hatred on Israel (*Ezekiel 28:25-26*). And we already know from the two previous chapters that the gathering of the Jews back in the land of Israel and the City of Jerusalem (as we see now) are events that precede the Second Coming of Jesus Christ. The reaction of Israel's neighbors to the gathering of those Jews is simply further confirmation that Jesus stands at the door.

CONCLUSION

The seemingly perpetual Arab-Israeli conflict is centered on a tiny sliver of land, less than one-tenth of one percent of the entire Middle East. Within that nation, all the focus is on a single city of 48.3 square miles.

Nevertheless, it's this real estate that commands the attention of the entire world. Despite the best efforts of her enemies, the Bible says Israel will never again be uprooted from the land God has given to the Jews (*Amos 9:13-15*).

I'll repeat that again, because it can't be overemphasized. There isn't going to be *another* dispersion and re-gathering of the Jewish people. The time of exile is over. The Jews are in Israel to stay. And if Israel is here to stay, then future wars waged against Israel will result in either a draw or further Israeli victory – just as we've seen time and again since 1948. But that won't always be clear in the world's eyes.

In yet another sign of the Second Coming, the Bible says that before Jesus returns, Israel will be the object of a surprise invasion. While Israel sits alone with no allies to defend her, the world will watch as a distinct alliance of nations moves in to destroy her. When I was born, this particular alliance of nations didn't exist. In fact, it had **never** existed.

But you know what? For the first time in all of recorded history, we see that alliance of future invaders coming together.

CHAPTER 8
SIGN #6: GOG OF MAGOG

IN 2001, IRANIAN President Muhammad Khatami became the first Iranian leader to visit Moscow since the 1979 revolution. His visit marked the continuation of closer relations between the two countries. Following the end of the Iran-Iraq War (1980-1988) and the death of Ayatollah Khomeini (1989), Iran and Russia steadily increased their economic and military ties, and Khatami's visit served to strengthen those ties.

In Moscow, he visited the Kremlin, where he met with Vladimir Putin and other top Russian political and military officials. The purpose? Increased cooperation in trade and military affairs, and a general increase in friendliness between the two nations.

Since Khatami's visit, Russia has agreed to sell arms to Tehran, renewed its 1995 commitment to help complete Iran's Bushehr nuclear reactor, and actively sought to curb United Nations sanctions against Iran over its nuclear ambitions. And as time goes by, the Russian-Iranian alliance will only grow stronger.

How can I be so sure? Because the Bible said so more than 2,000 years ago. And why should you care? Because the Bible said these same two nations will lead an alliance that will invade Israel just before Jesus returns. So if you're looking for a clue as to when the Second Coming will take place, you need to look for this alliance – an alliance which has never existed until now.

CHAPTER 8

THE GOG OF MAGOG INVASION

More than 2,600 years ago, the prophet Ezekiel warned of a future time when a vast coalition of nations will attack Israel. As this massive force invades, the entire world will watch – some in fear, some in anticipation. In the face of overwhelming odds, it will seem like Israel is all alone. Not a single nation will lift a finger to help her.

But you know what? Israel *isn't* alone. Because God says He will use this invasion to make Himself known to the entire world. All those people who have said, *"Where is God?"* and *"Why doesn't God reveal Himself?"* – those people will be silenced on that day. Because while the whole world watches, God Himself will destroy the Gog of Magog Alliance.

How do I know this? Because the Bible reveals the details of this future battle in the Book of Ezekiel, chapters 38 and 39. And again, this is the same Bible that has a perfect track record when it comes to fulfilled prophecy. Knowing this, I have 100% confidence that the Gog of Magog invasion will unfold just as the Bible says it will. So what does the Bible tell us?

The Bible tells us that the leader of this coalition is a man named Gog from the land of Magog. He's also known as the prince of Rosh, Meshech, and Tubal (***Ezekiel 38:2***). When Israel is living in peace, this man named Gog will come with a mighty army and cover the land like a cloud (***Ezekiel 38:14-16***). But his plans to conquer and pillage will come to nothing. Why? Because God promises to turn these enemy invaders against each other in combat (***Ezekiel 38:21***).

God says these invading armies will have their weapons knocked from their hands, and they will die in open fields where they'll become food for vultures and wild animals (***Ezekiel 39:3***).

In fact, the Bible says Gog's invasion of Israel will trigger an earthquake so strong every living creature on the face of the earth will tremble in God's presence (***Ezekiel 38:19-20***), and He will send a torrential rain of fire, hailstones, and burning sulfur on the invading armies (***Ezekiel 38:22***). The end result is the total destruction of the Gog of Magog Alliance. So many dead bodies will litter the landscape, it will take seven months to bury all the dead – even with the help of every citizen in Israel (***Ezekiel 39:12***).

Do you think that will get the world's attention? I think so. Once again, Israel will triumph in the face of overwhelming odds. But it won't be ingenious military plans or top secret weapons that defeat her enemies. Defeat will come from the hand of God Himself, and the whole world will know it.

Through His devastating response to the invading armies of the Gog of Magog Alliance, the God of Abraham, Isaac, and Jacob will announce His existence to a world that denies Him. Tired of being ignored, He promises to make His holy name known by saving the people of Israel, so the nations of the world will know that He alone is God (***Ezekiel 39:7; Ezekiel 38:16***).

And believe it or not, this entire chain of events is triggered when a man named Gog sets out to plunder the nation of Israel. But who is this man – this Gog of Magog? Where are the kingdoms of Rosh, Meshech, and Tubal? And who are his allies?

WHO ARE THE NATIONS IN THIS ALLIANCE?

Ezekiel identifies the nations in the Gog of Magog Alliance as "Magog, Rosh, Meschech, Tubal, Persia, Cush, Put, Gomer, and Beth-togarmah" (***Ezekiel 38:1-6***). I don't blame you at all if none of these names make any sense to you. After all, these don't sound like the names of any nations on earth today. But that doesn't mean that Ezekiel wasn't pointing to our day and time. In fact, as we'll see later, Ezekiel specifically states that this invasion will occur in our time.

Keep in mind that Ezekiel named the nations of this alliance as they were known in his day, and each one represents a clearly identifiable nation currently in existence. In fact, long before Russia became a world power, biblical scholars identified Rosh as the nation of Russia and Gog as its ruler.

The identity of Gog as the ruler of Russia is confirmed when Ezekiel notes his geographic location. Ezekiel says Gog will bring his armies from "the extreme north" (***Ezekiel 38:15; Ezekiel 39:2***). While this might seem like a broad statement rather than a specific prophecy, it's not. This statement, like most in the Old Testament, is made in reference to the nation of Israel. So it's saying that Gog will reside to the extreme north of Israel.

Draw a straight line north of Israel on any map of the Middle East, and guess what nation awaits? That's right – Russia. So Gog is clearly the ruler of Russia.

But Gog isn't alone. He has plenty of co-conspirators. Who are they? Below is the list of nations cited by Ezekiel. The Old Testament name is listed first, followed by its modern day equivalent:

Rosh = Russia

Magog = Kazakhstan, Uzbekistan, Turkmenistan, Kyrgyzstan, Tajikistan, and Afghanistan

Persia = Iran

Cush = Sudan

Put = Libya

Meshech, Tubal, Gomer, and Beth-togarmah = Turkey

Now, you might be thinking, "*Wait a minute Britt. This is a prime example of how you're reading into these 'prophecies.' These nations aren't called by name, but you claim Israel is! If all this is real, why doesn't the Bible clearly state 'Russia' and 'Iran' are part of this invading force? Why does it say Rosh and Persia?*"

My answer? It does.

Remember, these were the names of those countries back when Ezekiel recorded God's words. Since then, more than 2,500 years of human history passed. Nations changed, people intermarried, wars changed boundaries, old languages died, and new ones evolved. But you know what?

Israel is still around.

I'll go ahead and repeat that in case you overlooked the significance. Israel is still here – same name, same people, even though it went away for almost 2,000 years. This is a perfect illustration of why Israel is a modern day miracle. Where are these other Old Testament nations? Where are Magog, Meschech, and Tubal? Where are Persia, Cush, Put, and Gomer? They're still around, only with different names. And, in most cases, with different racial, cultural, and religious elements. Yet Israel remains.

It not only retains its ancient name, its people maintain the same national identity they had 2,600 years ago. Even though the Roman legions destroyed Israel, it came back. And even though Hitler tried to exterminate the Jews, his plan backfired and the Holocaust gave birth to the modern day nation of Israel. Against all odds, the Jewish people are back in the land. Do you think that's a mere coincidence? I don't.

Because God promised to gather His people back in the land of Israel, and God always keeps a promise.

THE HISTORY OF THE GOG OF MAGOG ALLIANCE

One such promise from God is that the Gog of Magog Alliance will one day attack the nation of Israel. In the history of the world, such an alliance of nations has never existed. But today we see it coming together right in front of us. Don't believe me? Just check your history books.

Up until March 21, 1935, the world knew the nation of Iran as Persia – the same Persia referenced in the Gog of Magog Alliance. In the 2,600 years since Ezekiel recorded his prophecies, the nations of Russia and Persia have never been part of an alliance of any sort. Economic and military cooperation between Persia (Iran) and Russia had never taken place – at least until around 1989.

But today? Iran and Russia are strong allies. For example, in 1995 the Russian Ministry for Atomic Energy signed an agreement with Iran to finish the Bushehr nuclear power plant. Construction on the plant had come to an immediate halt after the 1979 Islamic revolution. But today, thanks to Russia, work is once again in progress. The two nations continue to strengthen their economic and military ties, and Russia is one of the few world powers that consistently defends the existence of Iran's nuclear program.

Turkey is another interesting member of this military alliance. Since the restoration of Israel in 1948, those who understand bible prophecy have struggled to figure out how Turkey fits in.

Why?

Because in 1949, Turkey became the first Muslim majority country to officially recognize the state of Israel. Turkey and Israel have a long history of diplomatic, economic, and military cooperation. Turkey is also a member of NATO. And what is the purpose of NATO? Its purpose is to defend member nations against Russian aggression. So why would Turkey join a Russian alliance to invade another country?

While it hasn't made sense in recent years, that idea doesn't seem so far-fetched today. In May 2010, Turkey and Russia signed a series of agreements enhancing their energy ties, including an agreement to build Turkey's first nuclear power plant. And in recent years, Turkey's domestic politics – historically secular in nature – have been heavily influenced by Islam. And that gives Turkey more than enough motive to join the Gog of Magog Alliance.

Keep in mind that, with the exception of Russia, the contemporary nations in the Gog of Magog Alliance are majority Muslim nations. Kazakhstan, Uzbekistan, Turkmenistan, Kyrgyzstan, Tajikistan, and Afghanistan are all majority Muslim nations. Iran is 97% Muslim. Libya? 90%. Sudan? 97%. Today, most of these nations are antagonistic toward Israel. And the Bible says that soon, every one of them will be.

Does this surprise you? Again, it shouldn't. Because God revealed this more than 2,600 years ago, and He did more than simply tell us it would happen. He told us exactly *when* it would happen.

THE TIMING OF THE GOG OF MAGOG WAR

Prior to Gog's invasion, the nation of Israel will be at peace. It will be an unprotected nation without walls, confident in its security (*Ezekiel 38:11*). Think about that. In the days of Ezekiel, a city or a nation without walls was unheard of. It would have been a certain invitation for invasion.

But in the modern era of warfare, walls do little to repel an invading army. So while Israel today is a land guarded by walls, it's not a stretch at all to imagine a day in the near future when those walls are gone. In fact, that day is quickly approaching. How can I be so sure? Because the Bible tells us the precise time of the Gog of Magog invasion.

The Bible says this alliance will form and come against Israel "in the latter days" (*Ezekiel 38:8*). So what does that mean? Well, the key word in Hebrew is "acharith" which generally translates as the "after-part, latter part, last, close, or end." In other words, this alliance will form in the last days just prior to the return of Jesus Christ. Ezekiel uses this same word "acharith" again, when God says He will bring the alliance against the land of Israel "in the last days" (*Ezekiel 38:16*). And, at the beginning of verse 8, he reveals that this will happen "a long time from now" or "in the distant future." In other words, this is not a prophecy fulfilled in Ezekiel's day.

But that's not all he says. Ezekiel provides us with additional clues.

In fact, in the same passage cited above, God reveals precisely when this invasion will occur. In verse 12, Gog says to himself, "I will attack the once abandoned cities that are now populated with the Jews who returned from exile among the nations" (*Ezekiel 38:12*). Did you catch that? Gog will attack the land when it's filled with *the exiles who return from among the nations*. The target of Gog's invasion is modern day Israel.

God Himself confirms this when He says the invasion will occur "after Israel's people have been gathered from among many nations" (*Ezekiel 38:8*). He says it will happen "when I bring my people home from among the enemy nations" (*Ezekiel 39:27*). This return home from among many nations has happened only once in all of human history. And our generation is witness to that event – the 1948 gathering of the Jewish people and the restoration of Israel in the land ordained by God.

WHY IT MATTERS

So why do I think this a sign of the Second Coming? Well, we know from Chapter 5 of this book that the Old Testament prophets directly linked the restoration of Israel and the regathering of the Jewish people with the imminent coming of the Messiah. And Ezekiel links the Gog of Magog invasion with the restoration of Israel.

This means the appearance of the Gog of Magog Alliance is a necessary precursor to the Second Coming of Jesus Christ. So if the Second Coming is near, shouldn't we expect to see evidence of this alliance already forming? We should. And today, we do.

Never before in the history of the world has an alliance existed among the specific nations cited by Ezekiel. Yet today, we can clearly see the common interests shared by the nations he mentioned. This invasion requires a Russian-Iranian military alliance that didn't exist until recent times. In fact, Russian-Iranian cooperation of *any sort* had been for the most part non-existent until 1989. Today, Russia and Iran boast strong diplomatic, geopolitical, economic, and military ties. For the first time in the 2,600 years since Ezekiel recorded his prophecy, we see signs of the Gog of Magog Alliance coming together.

When you look at the world today, do you really think "things are the same now as they've always been"? I don't. Because the Bible says this alliance is a sign that the Second Coming is near, and I can see it forming in the daily news headlines. But you know what? It's not the only geopolitical alliance the Bible predicts for the last days. The scriptures say another specific alignment of nations is an even greater sign of Christ's return. And guess what? Today, we can see that alliance forming as well.

CHAPTER 9
SIGN #7: ROME REVIVED

MORE THAN 2,600 years ago, King Nebuchadnezzar of Babylon had a dream. Perplexed by its meaning, he commanded his royal astrologers and magicians to tell him what the dream meant. "No problem," they said. "What did you dream?"

But Nebuchadnezzar knew it would be a mistake to reveal his dream. After all, if the wise men in his court were so wise, they would know the meaning of the dream *and* what the dream was about. Right? Seems reasonable. So he refused to tell them his dream. And just as the king suspected, no one in the court could recount and interpret his dream.

But while none of the wise men in his court could perform this feat, one man in Babylon could. His name was Daniel. A slave taken captive from the conquered nation of Israel, Daniel worshipped the God of Abraham, Isaac, and Jacob.

"I can tell you your dream and its meaning," Daniel told the king. "Not because I'm wise, but because there's a God in heaven who reveals such things" (*Daniel 2:28*).

Daniel went on to describe the king's dream.

"You dreamed of a beautiful statue of a man with a head of gold, a chest and arms of silver, a belly and thighs of bronze, legs of iron, and feet made from a combination of iron and clay. A rock supernaturally cut from a mountain crushed the statue, and that rock became a great mountain covering the whole earth" (*Daniel 2:31-35*).

THE MEANING OF NEBUCHADNEZZAR'S DREAM

God revealed Nebuchadnezzar's dream to Daniel. But what did the dream mean? That's a good question, and fortunately for us, Daniel told the king. He explained that the statue represents a series of kingdoms. The first is Nebuchadnezzar's Babylon. So the statue's head of gold is a symbol of the kingdom of Babylon.

But when Nebuchadnezzar's kingdom comes to an end, another great kingdom will replace it. The chest and arms of silver are a symbol of this kingdom's power. In turn, a third kingdom will destroy the second kingdom. The bronze stomach and thighs represent this third kingdom.

A fourth kingdom will replace the third, and it will be as strong as iron. It will smash and destroy all the previous empires, and the legs of iron represent it.

The feet and toes made of iron and clay represent the final empire. Why iron and clay? Because this final empire will be an alliance of ten kingdoms, some strong like iron and some weak like clay. They will try to strengthen themselves by forming a union, but they will fail – just as iron and clay do not mix (*Daniel 2:38-43*).

Daniel's prophecy is more than twenty-six centuries old, and the historical record shows that all but one of these kingdoms (the last) has appeared and disappeared just as he predicted. Below is a list of the kingdoms from Nebuchadnezzar's dream:

1. Babylon
2. Medo-Persia
3. Greece
4. Rome
5. The Ten Nation Alliance

The first kingdom (the head of gold) was Nebuchadnezzar's Babylon. In 539 B.C., the Medo-Persian Empire (the chest and arms of silver) conquered Babylon. In 331 B.C., Alexander the Great defeated Darius in the battle of Gaugamela, and the Greek Empire (the bronze stomach and thighs) took control of Israel. Then, in 168 B.C., the Greek Empire fell to the Roman Empire (the legs of iron).

In the 4th Century, the Roman Empire split in two, with Rome as the center of power in the west and Constantinople as the center of power in the east. The statue's two legs of iron symbolize this split. In 476, Rome fell to Germanic invaders. Constantinople held out until 1453, when the Ottoman Turks conquered the city.

That leaves one kingdom remaining – the feet and toes of iron and clay. Where is this kingdom? And what do we know about it? We know from Daniel that it's a ten nation alliance. We also know it's composed of strong and weak members. Yet it will conquer the world before it's conquered itself. And the kingdom that destroys it will last forever.

The rock cut from the mountain represents this final, everlasting kingdom. It's the kingdom of Jesus Christ.

THE FOUR BEASTS

After Daniel interpreted Nebuchadnezzar's dream, the king installed Daniel as ruler of the province of Babylon and chief of all the wise men in his court (**Daniel 2:48**). Daniel interpreted other dreams for the king and served in his court for years.

After Nebuchadnezzar's death, God showed Daniel another vision. In this vision, Daniel saw four world empires, each represented by a beast (**Daniel 7:1-28**). An angel revealed that these four beasts represent four kingdoms (**Daniel 7:17**). In hindsight, we know that these four kingdoms are:

1. Babylon
2. Medo-Persia
3. Greece
4. Rome

Do these kingdoms look familiar? They should. They're the first four kingdoms represented in the statue. And the contrast between Daniel's vision and Nebuchadnezzar's dream reveal the difference between God's view of the world and humanity's view of the world. Why? Because in Nebuchadnezzar's eyes, these same kingdoms represent a beautiful statue. But in God's eyes, they represent horrible beasts.

The angel noted that the fourth beast (Rome) will be exceedingly powerful. All the previous governments represented in Nebuchadnezzar's statue will give way to this powerful world government.

Ten kings will rule this fourth kingdom. Different from the previous kingdoms, it will conquer the entire world and destroy everything in its path. Again, does this sound familiar? It should.

The ten toes on Nebuchadnezzar's statue represent the same ten kings who rule the fourth beast (***Daniel 2:41-43***). But Daniel 7 reveals something else. An eleventh king will come to power, subdue three of the ten kings, and consolidate power for himself (***Daniel 7:23-25***).

Given all this information, we have to ask ourselves a question. Does this fourth beast really represent Rome? After all, Rome achieved great power, but it never completely conquered the earth. And ten kings never jointly ruled the Roman Empire. Yet that's what Daniel 7 clearly describes.

So what does all this mean? It means exactly what it says. The Roman Empire, while ruled by ten kings, will conquer the entire earth. But the earth won't be conquered by the ***ancient*** Roman Empire. It will be conquered by a ***future*** Roman Empire.

That's right.

The Bible says the Roman Empire will come back. Think that's ridiculous? If so, just remember that the same Bible also predicted that Israel would come back.

Also remember that no fifth beast appears in Daniel's vision, and we know from history that the fourth beast is Rome. Why? Because it conquered the third beast in Daniel's vision (Alexander's divided Greek Empire), and history records that Rome conquered the remnants of Alexander's empire.

So Daniel's vision is telling us that the Roman Empire will come back. And when the Roman Empire comes back, ten kings will initially share power until a single king consolidates power over the entire kingdom. You've probably heard of this king before. He's known throughout the world, even by people who don't read the Bible. So what's his name?

His name is the Antichrist.

Knowing that the Antichrist will be the final kingdom's ruler, it makes sense that the fourth beast (Rome) is destroyed by the Second Coming of Jesus Christ (*Daniel 7:26-27*). In fact, when Jesus referred to Himself as the "Son of Man," He referenced this same vision where one like the Son of Man comes on the clouds of heaven, one whose rule is eternal and whose kingdom is everlasting (*Daniel 7:13-14, Mark 14:62*).

At the time of the Second Coming, Jesus isn't coming just to destroy the Antichrist, but to break forever the iron rule of the Antichrist's kingdom – a revived Roman Empire.

THE REVIVED ROMAN EMPIRE

Think I'm crazy? I can understand why you might think that, but neverthe-less, the Roman Empire *will* return – just as surely as Israel returned. How can I be so certain? Because the Bible declared it.

In fact, the nationality of the Antichrist serves as further confirmation that a revived Roman Empire is the final world power prior to the Second Coming. Why do I say this?

Because the Book of Daniel says the Antichrist will come from among the people whose armies destroy the City and the Temple (*Daniel 9:26*). And it specifically says when they will destroy the Temple. So when will it happen? *After the Messiah is killed* (*Daniel 9:26*).

And thanks to history, we know exactly when that happened. History reveals that the crucifixion of Jesus took place in A.D. 31. So did armies then come and destroy Jerusalem and the Temple? Yes. In A.D. 70, Titus led the Roman legions into Israel to put down an insurrection. This resulted in the destruction of Jerusalem and the Temple – just as Daniel predicted. And since Daniel stated that the Antichrist will come from among the people who destroy the City and the Temple, history confirms that the Antichrist will come from among the Roman people.

But the idea that the Roman Empire will return is not an idea confined to Daniel alone. The Book of Revelation says the same thing.

Toward the end of the first century, while exiled on the island of Patmos, John saw a vision of a woman sitting on a scarlet beast with seven heads and ten horns. Sounds weird, right?

Fortunately, as with Daniel, an angel revealed the true meaning to John. The seven heads represent seven kings, and the angel explicitly says, "five have fallen, the sixth reigns, and the seventh is yet to come – but his reign is brief" (***Revelation 17:9-10***). So who are these seven kings? They represent the seven kingdoms that have or will trample the nation of Israel. Historically, they are:

1. Egypt
2. Assyria
3. Babylon
4. Medo-Persia
5. Greece
6. Rome
7. The Revived Roman Empire

Remember, John wrote the Book of Revelation at the end of the first century, when the Roman Empire was at the height of its power. At that time, the first five kingdoms "had fallen," the sixth kingdom reigned (Rome), and the seventh was yet to come (the revived Roman Empire).

The beast itself represents the Antichrist and his kingdom, and its ten horns are ten kings who will one day rise to power and reign with the Antichrist. They will give all their power and authority to his kingdom – the revived Roman Empire (***Revelation 17:11-13***). These are the same ten kings symbolized by the feet and toes of iron and clay in Nebuchadnezzar's dream (***Daniel 2:41-43***).

As further confirmation that this final kingdom is a revived version of the Roman Empire, John describes the same beast in Revelation 13. He says one of the heads of the beast will seem wounded beyond recovery, but its fatal wound will be healed (***Revelation 13:3***). So what does this mean?

Well, think about it. If each head represents a kingdom, then what it's saying is that one of the kingdoms will appear to be destroyed, but it will come back to life. And we know from Daniel's description of the four beasts (***Daniel 7:1-28***) that the final kingdom is Rome. So John is telling us that the Roman Empire will be restored.

So if the Second Coming is close at hand, and the Bible says that Jesus Christ will destroy a revived version of the Roman Empire, shouldn't we see evidence or signs of this coming world kingdom? Shouldn't we see evidence that the Roman Empire is on the road to revival? Shouldn't we see evidence of weak and strong nations trying to strengthen themselves by forming an alliance? Yes, we should. And I don't think it's a coincidence we see those things happening today.

THE EUROPEAN UNION

In the aftermath of World War II, Europe lay in utter ruin. Many of its leaders believed that increased economic cooperation would significantly decrease the odds of another devastating war. The result? In 1950, the European Coal and Steel Community united six nations (Belgium, France, Germany, Italy, Luxembourg, and the Netherlands) under a single plan for managing their coal and steel industries.

The idea was that, under such an agreement, each nation would be unable to build weapons of war without the permission of the others. In addition, the agreement intertwined the best interests of each nation, making war less likely. This idea worked so well, the nations decided to expand it. In 1957, they signed the Treaty of Rome, creating the European Economic Community (EEC) and expanding cooperation into other economic sectors.

In 1973, three more nations (Denmark, Ireland, and the United Kingdom) joined the EEC. In the 1980s, Greece, Portugal, and Spain joined. Then, in a major step toward greater unification, the 1992 Maastricht Treaty replaced the EEC with the European Union (EU). The new treaty established parameters for a unified currency and foreign and security policy.

In 1999, the EU introduced the Euro. Actual Euro notes and coins were in circulation by 2002. Today, the EU includes 27 nations encompassing more than 500 million people.

Now, am I saying the European Union is the kingdom in Nebuchadnezzar's dream? No. At least not yet. But it does have some curious parallels. First, it encompasses Rome itself. That the treaty initiating the new super state is named the Treaty of Rome is no small detail. And many of the racial and cultural descendants of the Roman Empire live in the 27 nations that now comprise the EU.

But most importantly, the entire purpose of the European Union is to collectively strengthen the member nations through alliance – just as the statue's iron and clay feet and toes would attempt to strengthen themselves through "intermarriage" (*Daniel 2:43*).

According to Daniel, some parts of the alliance will be as strong as iron, while other parts will be as weak as clay. Does this describe the European Union? Absolutely!

As of 2013, the European Union contains the world's 4th, 5th, and 6th largest economies (Germany, France, and the United Kingdom) – but it also contains the world's 102nd, 121st, and 136th largest economies (Estonia, Iceland, and Malta). The European Union is literally a loosely connected confederation of nation states – some strong and some weak. And this is precisely the type of arrangement the Bible says will exist in the time just prior to Christ's return.

So why do I say this isn't necessarily the kingdom foreseen in Nebuchadnezzar's dream (at least as of right now)? Because the Bible says that ten kings will rule the revived Roman Empire. And right now, the European Union is not ruled by ten kings.

For a while, the ten member Western European Union (WEU) looked like a possibility. But it disbanded in 2011. Will a new ten nation council take its place? I don't know, and it's doubtful anyone will know until such an alliance emerges.

But what we do know is this: The framework currently exists for the emergence of a revived Roman Empire – an empire in the exact form Daniel foretold for the last days. How many generations over the past 2,600 years can make that same claim?

The answer is only one – *this generation*.

CONCLUSION

The Bible says that ten kings who rule a revived Roman Empire will cede their power to the Antichrist, a man who will rule as a global dictator for forty-two months (***Revelation 13:3-5***). Immediately after this three and a half year period, Jesus Christ will come back to earth and establish an everlasting Kingdom.

If it's true that the Second Coming is close at hand, we should see signs or clues of a revived Roman Empire on the horizon. So what do we see? Only this: While men of past generations tried to restore the Roman Empire through conquest (Charlemagne, Napoleon, and Hitler come to mind), ours is the only generation of the past 2,600 years positioned to fulfill the prophecies of Daniel and John.

Only now do we see strong and weak European nations joining in alliance. Only now do we see shadows of the European super state outlined in the scriptures.

The stage is set for a ten nation alliance of weak and strong nations to emerge in Western Europe. The European Union has a common currency and common diplomatic interests. And it's trending toward even greater political integration. According to the Bible, this is exactly what we'll see in the days and years leading up to the Second Coming.

Sometime soon, ten kings will emerge from the ashes of the Roman Empire. When they give their power to the Antichrist, the new Rome will consume everything in its path. It will be more powerful than any nation state in human history. And it won't just conquer its neighbors like previous empires. It will conquer every last square inch of the entire world.

CHAPTER 10
SIGN #8: GLOBAL GOVERNMENT

THE BOOK OF Genesis tells a famous story about the first ever attempt to form a world government. It's a well known story. Yet, it's not usually identified as a story about government. So what is this story? It's the story of the Tower of Babel.

Following the great flood, Noah's descendants repopulated the earth, and everyone spoke the same language (*Genesis 11:1*). National borders were non-existent, and cultural differences divided no one. As they moved eastward, some of the people settled in the land of Babylon.

"Come on," they told each other. "Let's collect bricks and build a great city with a tower that reaches into the heavens! This will keep us together and prevent us from scattering throughout the world" (*Genesis 11:2-4*).

But God looked down on this ambitious construction project and didn't like at all what He saw.

"Look at that," He said. "If a common language and political unity enable them to do this, imagine how powerful they'll become. I'll put a stop to this by giving them different languages. Then they won't be able to understand each other."

So God gave them different languages and scattered them across the earth, and the Tower of Babel project abruptly ended (*Genesis 11:5-9*).

For people who don't believe the Bible is the Word of God, the Tower of Babel is nothing more than a fairy tale, a story ancient man invented in order to explain different languages. And unfortunately, many Christians skim past this story as well. But remember, it's just as much a part of the Bible as the four Gospels or the Book of Acts.

So take a moment to think about this story. It's more than just a cute tale about an innocent tower. In fact, it speaks about a serious matter that impacts *you* today. Why do I say that? Because the story of the Tower of Babel is more than just a story, it's something else.

It's a prophecy.

That's right. The Tower of Babel is a prophecy of things to come. God looked down and saw mankind's attempt to form a world government, and He saw this prospect as so terrible and unacceptable that He put an immediate stop to it. But the Bible says something else as well. And what is it? It's that God won't restrain this global government forever.

THE COMING GLOBAL GOVERNMENT

The Bible tells us that the revived Roman Empire will be different from the kingdoms before it (*Daniel 7:7*) because it will be initiated by an alliance of ten kings and kingdoms. Babylon, Medo-Persia, Greece, or the Roman Empire of antiquity can't say that. But something else makes this future Roman Empire different.

What is it? It's that the revived Roman Empire will rule the entire earth (*Daniel 7:23*). Did you catch that? In case you didn't, I'll repeat it again because it's extremely important. It's vital to understanding what the Bible has to say about the end times.

The revived Roman Empire will rule *the whole world*. No kingdom on earth will be able to stand against it. It will destroy all opposition in its path. This not only makes it different from the past kingdoms and empires of the world, it makes it completely unique.

Egypt, Assyria, Babylon, Medo-Persia, Greece, Rome – all these kingdoms and empires were powerful, but they were still regional powers. Sure, the ancient Roman Empire was vast and influential, but it didn't rule China. It didn't rule South America. It ruled a significant portion of the known world, but it wasn't a *global* empire. And that's what makes the revived Roman Empire so different.

The revived Roman Empire will rule every trace of soil on the planet. Every drop of water in every lake, river, and ocean. Nothing on earth will escape its authority. It will rule the world politically (***Revelation 13:7***), religiously (***Revelation 13:8***), and economically (***Revelation 13:16-17***). The power of this empire will be so immense, the people of the world will actually ***worship*** it like a god. "Who else is this great?" they'll say. "What nation on earth – what people – can oppose it?" (***Revelation 13:4***).

In the Book of Revelation, John describes the power of this kingdom and its ruler, the Antichrist, saying they will rule over "all people, tribes, and languages" on the face of the earth (***Revelation 13:7***). The authority of this new Roman Empire will be so all-encompassing that no one will be able to buy or sell anything without its permission (***Revelation 13:16-17***). This is an awesome and unprecedented power – the power to control all economic activity and literally shut down black markets. Such a power has never existed in history, and it doesn't exist as of the writing of this book. Yet the Bible says it will come.

So when will it come? The Bible tells us that too. The revived Roman Empire's global dominance will begin three and a half years prior to the Second Coming of Jesus Christ (***Daniel 7:25***). For those three and a half years, the Antichrist will use his kingdom's unprecedented authority to rule the world, and his power will only be broken when Jesus returns to establish His kingdom – a kingdom that will last forever (***Daniel 7:27***).

In other words, if the return of Jesus is near, we should see signs of a coming global government right now. Is that what we see?

OUR WORLD TODAY

Since the Tower of Babel, nationalism, borders, different languages, and diverse cultures have prevented world government. But unfortunately, we see the deterioration of those obstacles today. The world views this as a good thing. But as the Tower of Babel story reveals, the world's view is the opposite of God's view.

Nevertheless, despite the historical absence of a world government, the Bible insists one is coming. And we can see the initial signs of its arrival in our day and time. Our first glimpse arrived in the aftermath of World War I, when world leaders formed the League of Nations in an attempt to establish world peace and cooperation. When that didn't work, and World War II left Europe in ruins, many of those same world leaders created the United Nations.

Today, we can see the framework of a future global government in the structure of the United Nations. The UN maintains its own International Court of Justice, its own military forces, its own environmental policies, and its own disaster relief efforts. And there's a big push to give the United Nations the power to tax.

Free trade agreements like the North American Free Trade Agreement (NAFTA) and alliances like the European Union facilitate open borders, and the Internet destroys many of the remaining barriers. Totalitarian states like Iran and China used to be able to shut out most outside influence, and they still have considerable power to censor. But that power isn't 100% effective, and the Internet is exposing their citizens to outside voices.

Even language barriers, which divided people at the Tower of Babel, will soon disappear. Today, English is spoken in most countries, and international collaboration is common. But soon, new technologies will enable us to eliminate language barriers forever. People will speak in their native language and, through a special earpiece, be heard in the listener's native language. It's only a matter of time, and once it happens, the language barrier will disappear forever.

In the past, distinct cultures erected barriers between nations, creating an obstacle to a sense of common ground. But with the rise of modern technology, we see cultural barriers disappearing too. Regional and national cultures melt together with on-demand, anywhere streaming of movies, music, books, and websites. We have global sports stars, global movie stars, and global musicians. And all of this contributes to the development of one global culture.

Nationalism is on its deathbed due to a dramatic increase in education and international travel. Fewer and fewer people buy into the notion that their country is superior or always right. And more and more people view themselves as "citizens of the world."

Of particular note is the breakdown of nationalism in favor of a greater Europe in the nations of the European Union. The Bible claims this general geographic area will give rise to the revived Roman Empire and a global dictatorship. And the EU is reflective of other regions in the world, where trade flows freely across borders and we see the gradual elimination of cultural and linguistic barriers.

THE ENORMITY OF SUCH A CLAIM

The prospect of a world government doesn't seem so far-fetched today. In fact, many world leaders openly dream about it. But think for a moment about the enormity of this claim, especially when made by God's prophets anywhere from 1,900 to 2,600 years ago. When Daniel and John said a revived Roman Empire would rule the world, they did so at points in time when no one in the world knew with any certainty how many continents were in the world, much less how many people or nations existed.

So the idea of a truly global government, especially one that controlled all commerce, **was** far-fetched. In the days of Daniel and John, a true global empire was impossible. Imagine the ancient Roman Empire – even with all its power and might – administering a global government. Talk about a bureaucratic nightmare! Such an empire would stretch armies, supply lines, and communications razor thin and its influence would weaken with each step you took away from its command and control center – Rome.

But even if the ancient Roman Empire could have managed the organizational challenges of a global empire, do you really think it could have controlled every economic transaction in a global economy? Of course not. The Roman Empire couldn't even control every economic transaction in the

City of Rome itself. Black markets were alive and well in ancient Rome, and they're alive and well today. But a day will soon come when black markets no longer exist, because the Bible says the revived Roman Empire will be so powerful no one will be able to buy or sell anything without its permission (***Revelation 13:17***).

How is this possible? It's difficult to say. But the most likely explanation is through exponential increases in the power of technology. Already, the majority of the world's financial transactions are electronic, and governments can see and track everything. Cash-only black markets do exist, but in time, the proliferation of near-free, ubiquitous cameras and listening devices will cover the entire globe. And when that happens, nothing will escape the eyes of Big Brother.

CONCLUSION

The Bible clearly states that just prior to the Second Coming of Jesus Christ, a global government will dominate the world. Yet, for all of human history, global government has not only been elusive, it's been impossible. Today, it's not only becoming possible. It's a foregone conclusion.

Oddly, this is a sign of the Second Coming that most people tend to overlook. Why? Because they can't see the forest for the trees. They're standing on the exponential curve, and they fail to see the unique position of this generation in the great timeline of human history.

For the first time ever, global government is possible. But why? Is it because world leaders are afraid the next war will be the last, and they're eager to cooperate? Is it because this generation is more unified than previous generations? Is it because people now view themselves as "world citizens"? No. These are all good reasons. But only one thing makes world government possible for the first time since the Tower of Babel – human technological advancement.

CHAPTER 11
SIGN #9: ADVANCED TECHNOLOGY

WHEN APOLLO II's Eagle landed on the moon, the world watched in amazement as two astronauts opened the door and descended a ladder. Then Neil Armstrong set foot on the moon and made his famous "small step" quotation. The rest, as they say, is history.

Nevertheless, within a year, landing on the moon was old news. Commonplace, run-of-the-mill news. Apollo 12 launched and did the same thing. So when Apollo 13 launched on April 11, 1970, few people paid any attention. Of course, that quickly changed as an oxygen tank explosion threatened to ruin the mission and strand three men in outer space. But they made it home, and space travel once again became routine.

So what's my point? Only this – the pace of technological change is not only rapid, it's expected. We've become so conditioned to expect the miraculous that we fail to grasp how truly astounding our technology is. What we have today is unprecedented in human history, and we take it for granted.

That's why it's not surprising that so many people overlook the rapid pace of technological advancement as a sign of the Second Coming. People are immune to its wonders. They think humans have always lived this way. This is why so many people can say with a straight face, *"Why do you think Jesus is coming back? People have been saying that for years, yet look around you, the world's the same as it's always been."*

Only it's not.

The world is far from "the same as it's always been." And one reason why is our advanced technology. For centuries, the human race realized slow and incremental advances in technology. But the past two hundred years have brought an explosion in technological growth.

You probably agree. However, we may not agree when I state this is just one more reason to believe Jesus is coming soon.

"But Britt," you might say. *"How is advanced technology a sign of the Second Coming? The Bible doesn't directly mention modern technologies like computers, TV, radio, and modern weapons. In fact, it may not mention them at all."*

That's true. But there's substantial evidence to believe that today's technological advancements foreshadow the fulfillment of specific bible prophecies – bible prophecies slated for fulfillment just prior to the Second Coming.

WHY ADVANCED TECHNOLOGY IS A SIGN

Ours is the first generation with (or about to acquire) technologies that can fulfill many of the Bible's end time prophecies. In fact, the Book of Revelation describes several key end time events that, outside of supernatural intervention, require advanced technology for fulfillment. Some of these technologies already exist. Others will be developed in the near future.

Now, don't get me wrong. The fulfillment of God's Word isn't dependent on human efforts. All of these signs could (and can) be fulfilled supernaturally. So why do I bring it up? Because ours is the first generation capable of fulfilling these prophecies **without** the need for supernatural intervention. Don't you find that interesting? I do.

For the first time ever, these signs can be fulfilled with existing human technology. Here are just a few examples:

Control Over All Financial Transactions – According to the Bible, the Antichrist will require every person on earth to receive a mark on the right hand or forehead. Without this mark, they won't be able to buy or sell anything (*Revelation 13:16-17*).

Think about that for a minute. Everyone in the entire world will receive a mark. And without it, they won't be able to buy or sell anything. Not some things or certain things. *Anything*.

Clearly, this passage says that the Antichrist will control all the financial transactions in the world. This means that black markets will no longer exist. And we're not at that point today. After all, drug dealers and terrorist organizations routinely hide their financial transactions from government authorities.

But when this absolute economic control arrives, how will it even be possible? Control over every economic transaction in the world requires the means to monitor those transactions. And that's a monumental task, right? Yet we already live in a world where governments routinely monitor financial transactions. Don't believe me? Try hiding your income from the IRS. Even if you have a Swiss bank account, it won't be long before they come knocking on your door.

For centuries, economic activity thrived on barter and currency transactions. But today, currency is used less and less. The overwhelming majority of all financial transactions are electronic. But despite this arrangement, we don't see the type of absolute worldwide control predicted in the Bible. However, that's quickly changing.

The widespread use of electronic devices, cameras, and microphones is increasing at breakneck speed. A time will soon come when "smart dust" technology will enable an all-powerful world government to see, hear, record, and analyze everything. Every conversation. Every encounter. Every transaction. Orwell's Big Brother is coming, and when he arrives, you won't be able to hide anything from the watchful eye of government.

The Whole World Watching – The Bible says that during the Tribulation, God will send two witnesses to preach His message to the world. These two witnesses will have supernatural powers such as the power to breathe fire, the power to stop rain, the power to turn rivers and oceans into blood, and the power to strike the earth with plagues (*Revelation 11:3-6*).

After they finish preaching, the Antichrist will kill these two witnesses and leave their bodies in the streets of Jerusalem (*Revelation 11:7-8*). Then, something truly amazing will happen.

For three and a half days, ***all the people in the world*** will stare at their bodies (*Revelation 11:9*).

Go ahead and read that again, because it's a truly remarkable statement. The Bible says everyone in the entire world will stare at the dead bodies of these two men. But how? Will the entire world pass single-file through the City of Jerusalem over the course of three and a half days? Probably not.

So how will the entire world stare at them? When John recorded the Book of Revelation in the first century, there wasn't any other way. But today we know there is. With modern satellite television and mobile devices connected to the Internet, watching events from other parts of the world is routine and commonplace. In fact, just like men on the moon, it's something we've come to expect.

That said, the idea of watching events unfold in real-time on the other side of the earth is still a new thing when compared to the long course of human history.

Remember, this statement was first written almost 2,000 years ago. At that time, looking at something firsthand was the only way to see it. There were no photographs. No movies. No television. Nothing but firsthand experience.

Maybe you could catch a glimpse of a scene on a mosaic, mural, or tapestry. But scenes captured in works of art are a far cry from "staring" at reality as it unfolds, and that's exactly what the Bible says will happen in the end times.

For more than 1,700 years after John recorded the Book of Revelation, firsthand experience was the only way you could witness an event. But today? Not only do we have pictures and recorded video, but we can watch live events on mobile devices. And the cost of this technology will continue to decrease, eventually giving Third World nations the same instantaneous access we enjoy today.

The result of all of this? For the first time in history, it will be possible for the entire world to simultaneously view an event anywhere in the world

– just as the Book of Revelation predicts. This fact alone serves as strong evidence that our generation is on the cusp of Christ's return.

Flesh on the Verge of Disappearing – When His followers asked Jesus to tell them the signs of His coming and the end of the age, He described the time just before His arrival and said, "Unless those days are shortened, no flesh will survive" (*Matthew 24:22*).

But what does this mean? Does it mean that everyone will die? It could. It could well mean that unless Jesus returns at that precise moment, a final world war will erupt and the human race will destroy itself. In fact, this is the traditional interpretation. But is it correct? In my next book, I'll make the case that it means something far more sinister.

But regardless of the ultimate meaning, the idea that humanity is on the brink of annihilation is relatively new. While the 14th Century outbreak of bubonic plague killed an estimated one-third of humanity, it didn't come close to killing *everyone*.

In the nearly 2,000 years since Jesus spoke those words, the world has witnessed countless wars, famines, epidemics, plagues, and natural disasters. Yet almost thirty times as many people inhabit the earth today as lived when Jesus made His statement. For more than 1,900 of those years, the world experienced "business as usual."

But all that changed in 1945. Following detonation of the first atomic bomb, humanity entered the nuclear age. Within a decade, the world's great powers – the United States and the Soviet Union – found themselves locked in a Cold War, both armed to the teeth with nuclear weapons. How many nuclear weapons? Enough to destroy the world.

According to the Bible, fire will one day consume a third of the earth, trees and grass (*Revelation 8:7*). Some think this is supernatural fire – the result of God's judgment. And it may well be. But starting in the mid-20th Century, humanity acquired the power to cause the same type of destruction on its own. That's a notable development, don't you think? I do.

In fact, back in October 1962, the world stood on the brink of nuclear annihilation. Think about that. Humanity almost destroyed itself in 1962.

How many generations can say that? Not many. Only those alive from around 1945 to the present have been able to credibly claim it's even *possible* for humanity to destroy itself. Does that sound like a world where "things are the same as they've always been"?

UNIQUE IN HISTORY

While the Tribulation features supernatural acts by both God and Satan, ours is the first generation capable of fulfilling many of the Book of Revelation's prophecies **without** a need for supernatural feats.

This is one of the strongest arguments in favor of the imminent return of Jesus Christ. However, it's also one of the least accepted because it's difficult for people living in our time to recognize just how completely unique and unrecognizable our world is when compared to previous generations. But if you take the time to study and examine human history, it's clear that Jesus is knocking on the door.

Would it have been realistic for the whole world to literally watch an event unfold prior to our generation? Of course not, yet it would seem like business as usual today.

Was it realistic to believe a single individual could control all world commerce prior to our generation? Of course not, yet our generation is the first to conduct the majority of its financial transactions electronically. Is it really so crazy to believe a single, centralized government could one day take control over all those transactions? I don't think so.

Would it have been realistic for a previous generation to create a giant worldwide database containing the financial history of every single individual on earth who accepted a mark? Of course not. Any attempt to implement such a system, without the aid of powerful computers and sophisticated software, would result in a bureaucratic nightmare of inefficiency.

And monitoring all financial transactions? Impossible without computer technology. Yet today, it's not inconceivable that such a system could exist. Why? Because of advanced computer technology.

Because of our technology, many end time prophecies which once baffled biblical scholars aren't so baffling anymore. With the use of modern technology, we can see how those prophecies could be fulfilled.

In fact, in some cases, we see the literal fulfillment of bible prophecy through the use of advanced technology. What fulfilled prophecy am I talking about? One that Jesus said is a necessary precursor to His return. Jesus said that once we see this sign, **the end will come**. And you know what? You're witnessing its fulfillment right before your eyes.

CHAPTER 12
SIGN #10: WORLDWIDE PREACHING OF THE GOSPEL

FOR MUCH OF human history, a book took many weeks or months to copy by hand. And the cost to buy one? Enormous. But it didn't matter anyway because most people were illiterate. But today? Billions are literate, and books spread like wildfire at minimal cost.

For example, in all likelihood, you're reading this book on an e-reader device. The cost to buy it? Less than half of what it would cost as a paperback. And believe it or not, that's expensive!

My book *Coming To Jesus: One Man's Search for Truth and Life Purpose* is regularly given away for free, and as technology advances, it will be seamlessly translated into every language in the world and end up in the hands of everyone on the planet who wants it. That's where we're headed. A time when information will be abundant and affordable for everyone – not just those in the Western world.

So why do I bring this up? Only to point out how dramatically different our world is. After all, it hasn't always been this way. And the recent explosion in communication technology is enabling the fulfillment of one of the primary signs of the Second Coming.

CHAPTER 12

A SIGN OF HIS COMING

What is this sign? It's a sign that's moving toward fulfillment right before our eyes. It's the spread of the Gospel to the farthest corners of the earth.

Nearly 2,000 years ago, the disciples asked Jesus to reveal the signs of His coming and the end of the age. In other words, when will His Kingdom arrive and when will our suffering under the injustice of worldly government end?

Jesus described many signs to look for. But among them, He said this, "And the Gospel will be preached throughout the entire world, so that every nation will hear it – *and then the end will come*" (***Matthew 24:14***).

Think we're getting close to that day now? I do. The Bible is available in thousands of languages. Satellites broadcast Christian programming throughout the world, and every day, missionaries carry the Gospel to people who have never heard it before. Yet, we're still not there.

That said, the day will come. According to the Bible, it will come during the Tribulation. The Book of Revelation claims that every nation, tribe, language, and people will hear the good news of Jesus Christ (***Revelation 14:6***).

Again, Jesus said, "And the Good News of the Kingdom will be preached throughout the whole world, so that every nation will hear it – *and then the end will come*" (***Matthew 24:14***).

Notice what Jesus *didn't* say. He didn't say the Gospel will be preached to the whole world for the second time or the third time. And He didn't say the Gospel will be preached to the whole world for a period of 50 or 100 years. It's implied that once the Gospel is preached to the whole world, *then the end will come.*

In other words, once the whole world hears the Gospel, that's it. Jesus is coming.

A BOLD PREDICTION

Think about that for a moment. That's a bold prediction, don't you think? Jesus said that ***all nations*** will hear the Gospel of His Kingdom. Due to the benefit of hindsight, most people today shrug this off as no big deal. After all, the Gospel is everywhere – right?

But remember, Jesus made this proclamation in the early first century – almost 2,000 years ago. At best, He had several thousand followers at the time, and the overwhelming majority of those followers were Jews living in Israel. Few ever traveled outside of the region.

There were no films of His miracles, and the Sermon on the Mount was not broadcast.

We do know that some Greeks in the Book of John asked about Him, so word of Jesus certainly traveled (*John 12:20*). But the world was a big place. Certainly the people of China, Japan, North America, South America, and most of Africa had never heard of Jesus. In fact, the people of Israel were totally unaware that entire continents existed. North America. South America. Australia. Antarctica. These were all unknown places.

So the idea that a carpenter and some fishermen could spread a message to the ends of the earth was a bold claim – some would say, an impossible claim. Yet, that's exactly what we see today.

THE MODERN TOOL OF EVANGELISM

For hundreds of years after the ministry of Jesus, the Word of God could be spread in only two ways – word-of-mouth and handwritten messages such as letters. Christians could share the written word, but they had to copy it by hand. And this was usually an expensive, time consuming and labor intensive process. Not exactly the most efficient way to reach a mass audience.

Yet, through the efforts of the apostles "to go forth and spread the Gospel," the Good News of Jesus Christ made its way through the surrounding regions of Judea. The perfect example of this early evangelism is exhibited in the life of Paul. Following his conversion on the road to Damascus, Paul took the Gospel throughout the northern Mediterranean region – to Turkey, Greece, and finally Rome itself.

But after 1,600 years of evangelism, Christianity was largely confined to Europe, Western Asia, and North Africa. Its influence didn't touch every part of the globe.

So if Christian evangelists couldn't bring the Gospel to every corner of the earth after 1,600 years, how could the Book of Revelation claim that the Gospel will be preached to every nation, tribe, people, and language within the short seven year period of the Tribulation?

How does the Gospel reach so many people in such a short period of time? While we won't know for sure until it happens, we can make an educated guess. My best guess? Technology. With modern technology, a single individual can simultaneously preach the Gospel of Jesus Christ to billions of people.

REACHING THE WORLD

In 1934, Christian evangelist Mordecai Ham held a revival meeting in Charlotte, North Carolina. Among the many people who committed their lives to Jesus Christ that day was a teenager named Billy Graham. Maybe you've heard of him? After all, Billy Graham is one of the most famous Christian evangelists in all of history.

Certainly, Mordecai Ham was an effective advocate for Jesus Christ, but he could only reach so many people with the Gospel. The size of his audience was limited to how many people could fit in a tent revival. Ham could reach his largest audience on radio, but even those radio broadcasts had a limited audience size.

Contrast this with Billy Graham's career. Graham's ministry came of age when the era of television exploded onto the scene. Millions of people viewed his revival meetings on prime time television, and Graham recorded his sermons and crusades. Today, his ministry – the Billy Graham Evangelistic Association – broadcasts on TV, radio, and the Internet. On YouTube, you can watch hundreds and hundreds of Billy Graham sermons, sermons that are just as timeless as when they were first preached. The result? Billy Graham will continue to bring people to Jesus Christ until the end of the age.

And Billy Graham isn't alone.

Today, you can see Billy Graham "Crusade Classics" on the Trinity Broadcasting Network (TBN). Paul Crouch founded the network with a single station back in 1973. Today, more than five dozen satellites beam TBN to thousands of television stations all over the world with programming in dozens and dozens of languages. And TBN continues to expand its reach into new territories. And guess what? TBN isn't alone. A number of Christian television networks are available via cable and satellite with signals reaching all over the world.

In 1989, Todd Strandberg started what would later become the Rapture Ready website by making weekly postings to Internet newsgroups. In 1995, he repackaged his posts as a website featuring just seven articles. Today, the Rapture Ready website hosts more than 30,000 articles and reaches more than 400,000 unique visitors per month. And like TBN, Rapture Ready isn't alone. It's just one of thousands of websites with a global audience.

And you know what? As language translation software improves, and more and more people connect to the Internet, this audience will continue to grow. What's amazing is that, like Billy Graham's recorded sermons, an article written ten years ago continues to reach people today.

In 2008, LifeChurch.tv launched YouVersion, a free Bible app featuring more than 600 translations in more than 400 languages. As of this writing, it's been downloaded more than 100 million times. As smart phone, eReader, and mobile device users grow in number, free apps enable the Gospel to reach almost everyone on the face of the earth. Do you think all of this is more evidence that today is "the same as it's always been?"

Growing up, I remember my brother showing me a television program featuring a remote tribe of Aboriginal people who lived in the Australian Outback. They were isolated from western society, and I was fascinated by these people who lived their lives virtually unchanged from the ways of their ancestors. They were untouched by the trappings of modern society and the wonders of the industrial revolution.

Today? Those same Aborigines have cell phones.

APPROACHING THE END

As technology climbs the exponential curve, the number of methods for transmitting the Gospel will increase exponentially. Satellite and cable television programs, websites, podcasts, mobile apps, physical books, eBooks, movies, email, printed materials, live gatherings, and dozens of other mediums enable the message of Jesus to saturate the globe.

As technology advances, we'll soon reach the point where every individual has readily available access to the Good News of Jesus Christ. And then? Jesus says *"and then the end will come"* (**Matthew 24:14**).

CONCLUSION

According to Jesus, the preaching of His message "throughout the whole world" will precede His return.

Yet, in the first century, the teachings of Jesus were confined to a relatively small number of people in and around Israel. And much of the earth's land mass was completely unknown to the disciples of Jesus, so the odds of the disciples preaching the Gospel of Christ "throughout the whole world" were quite remote.

Yet, 2,000 years later, the Gospel is preached in every nation, the Bible is translated in thousands of languages, and the Good News of Jesus Christ is delivered through thousands of ministries via radio, cable TV, satellite, the Internet, and countless other technologies of mass communication.

Is this "the way it's always been?"

Nope.

But that's what Peter's scoffers would have us believe. The truth is our generation is closer to preaching the Gospel "throughout the whole world" than any preceding generation. And according to Jesus, that fact alone should grab your attention.

CHAPTER 13
SIGN #11: CONVERGENCE

J UST DAYS BEFORE His crucifixion, Jesus and his disciples were visiting
the Temple in Jerusalem. Impressed by what they saw, the disciples pointed
out the majesty and craftsmanship of the Temple structures. But Jesus? His
reaction was quite different.

"You see these stones?" Jesus said. "The day will come when not one
of these stones will be left on top of another."

This surprised the disciples. Curious, they asked Him, "Lord, when will
all this take place? What signs should we look for to tell us you're coming?"

Jesus went on to describe a series of signs and events they should look
for. And the grand finale of all these events? Jesus said, "Then everyone in
the world will see the Son of Man coming on the clouds in great power and
glory" (*Luke 21:27*).

But what did Jesus mean when He said this?

Jesus was referring to the Book of Daniel and its description of a
Messiah who will come to earth and rule the world forever (*Daniel 7:13*).
This passage is a description of His Second Coming. Later, Jesus made this
reference again when He told the high priest Caiaphas and the Sanhedrin
that they would see Him "coming on the clouds of heaven" (*Matthew 26:64*).

The signs Jesus revealed to His disciples (*Luke 21:5-36*) are signs that
will precede His Second Coming. Jesus told His disciples to look for these

signs, and He told them they will appear at a specific point in time – a time when all these signs will appear at once.

According to Jesus, these aren't generic signs, but specific signs unique to the generation in which they occur. This book has examined many of the signs – signs cited by both Jesus and the Old Testament prophets. And each and every one of these signs is unique to our generation. At the dawn of the 20th Century, *not a single one* was present. Now they all are.

Doesn't that make you curious? It should. After all, Jesus told His disciples point blank that when you see these signs, you should look up. Why? *Because that's when He's Coming.*

WHAT ARE THE ODDS?

Jesus commanded His followers to look for these signs. He said when you see them, His return is near. So what did He mean by "near"? Jesus specifically used the phrase "right at the door." But again, what does that mean? It means His return is imminent. It could come at any moment.

Alone, each of the signs we've examined indicate the Second Coming of Jesus Christ is near. But the appearance of all these signs *at the same time*? That should convince you beyond all doubt. After all, what are the odds?

For instance, in the Book of Revelation, John describes a 200 million man army (*Revelation 9:16*). In the late first century, when John recorded Revelation, experts estimate this was close to the entire world population. So the idea of a 200 million man army was laughable in the first century. But today? Not so much. Alone, China and India each have over a billion people.

Now, guess where John said these armies would come from? He said the Euphrates river will dry up so "kings of the east" can travel through with their armies (*Revelation 16:12*). Of course, if you know your world geography, you know that both China and India are east of the Euphrates River.

Is this just another coincidence? Is it just random chance that a 200 million man army is possible at the same moment in time when every sign of the Second Coming is present? I don't think so, and you shouldn't either.

Think about it. God is speaking to our generation. Jesus commanded us to look for the very signs we see today. Don't you think we should pay attention?

Take a step back and look at each sign. What do you think the odds are each of these signs would appear based on random chance alone?

1) **The Jews in Israel** – The Jews are back in Israel. God foretold this modern miracle through His prophets – Isaiah, Jeremiah, Ezekiel, and Jesus Himself. What are the odds random chance resulted in the rebirth of an ancient nation? How many ancient nations reappear hundreds of years after their complete destruction? And not just reappear with the same name, but retain their distinct racial, cultural, and religious heritage?

   At best, you're looking at a long shot. In fact, it's only happened *twice* in all of human history. That's right. It's such a rare occurrence that it's only happened twice in all of recorded history. The most recent case is one we've already examined – Israel in 1948. But what about the other case?

   It shouldn't surprise you when I say that it was Israel. Around 1500 B.C., Moses led the Hebrew slaves out of Egypt, and they eventually resettled the land of Abraham, Isaac, and Jacob. Think that's a coincidence? I don't.

   Over and over, the Old Testament prophets linked the return of the Jews and the rebirth of Israel with the end of the age. And Jesus said this sign will precede His Second Coming. Yet for 1,878 years of Christianity, this sign wasn't anywhere to be seen. Today, it's in your daily headlines.

2) **The Jews in Jerusalem** – Israel controls Jerusalem. According to Jesus, Daniel, and Zechariah this is a necessary precursor to the Second Coming. Zechariah said the Jewish people will once again play in the streets. Today, they do. Don't think this is a big deal?

   Remember, for 1,897 years this wasn't the case. From A.D. 70 to June 7, 1967, the Jewish people had **zero** control over Jerusalem. They were scattered around the world. Today, they're not only back in the land, but in the Old City of Jerusalem itself.

3) **The Exponential Curve** – Jesus said just before His return, the world will experience "birth pains." In other words, certain events will increase in both frequency and intensity. What specific events did He mention? Wars, rumors of wars, famines, earthquakes, false messiahs, and a number of other events. Do we see this today? We do.

Far more people died from 20th Century wars and famines than lived on the entire earth in the first century.

4) **Increased Travel and Knowledge** – According to the Book of Daniel, travel and knowledge will increase significantly in the time just prior to the Second Coming. And that's exactly what we see today.

For the first 1,600 years of Christianity, our ability to travel and the base of human knowledge remained relatively unchanged. But the Industrial Revolution unleashed exponential change. In the mid-19th Century, traveling from New York to San Francisco was an arduous, multi-month journey. Today, it's a few hours in a plane.

5) **A European Confederation** – Both Daniel and John said a loose confederation of European states will appear in the end times. This ten nation alliance will take over the world, and only the Second Coming of Jesus Christ will destroy the global empire they create. Daniel said this alliance will include both weak and strong nations, and these nations will fit together poorly, just as iron and clay don't mix.

Do we see this today? We don't see the ten nation alliance yet. But we do see a loose confederation of European states. And just as Daniel foretold, the European Union consists of both weak and strong states. Is this just another coincidence?

6) **A Russian-Iranian Alliance** – According to Ezekiel, a Russian/Iranian-led coalition of nations will attack Israel in the last days. Soon thereafter, the Second Coming will take place. Ezekiel said this in 600 B.C. From his time until well into the 20th Century, such an alliance **never** existed. Today, it does.

Russia and Iran are now allies. In fact, they're two of the most powerful players in Middle East politics. And both are aligned against Israel. Coincidence?

7) **Israel's Hostile Neighbors** – The Old Testament prophets revealed that after the rebirth of Israel, the hostility of her neighboring nations will boil over. They'll say "Come, let us wipe away the nation of Israel. Let's destroy the memory of its existence" (***Psalm 83:4***). And they'll say, "Let us take for ourselves these pasturelands of God" (***Psalm 83:12***).

   And when does the Bible say this will happen? Right before Jesus comes back. Do we see this today? Do I even have to ask that question? This is all we've seen since 1948. But for almost nineteen centuries before that, this sign didn't exist.

8) **Advanced Technology** – When an angel showed Daniel various end times events, Daniel struggled to understand (***Daniel 12:8***). He asked what it all meant. The response? The angel told Daniel "all these things are kept secret until the time of the end" (***Daniel 12:9***). But why? Why couldn't Daniel understand what he saw?

   He couldn't understand because the world was so dramatically different. If Daniel had looked ahead to the first century, do you think he would have been confused? Probably not. First century life wasn't much different from his own world. What if he caught a glimpse of life in the 5th Century? 10th Century? 15th Century? For thousands of years, society stayed more or less the same. Only in the 19th and 20th Centuries would Daniel encounter a more complex world that strained his understanding.

   Why? Advanced technology has dramatically changed our world. Imagine living 2,600 years ago. An angel appears and shows you visions of skyscrapers, jet airplanes, satellites, iPhones, etc. Wouldn't you be confused?

9) **Global Government** – According to the Book of Revelation, a global empire will rule the world in the years just before Jesus returns. And while a global government doesn't exist yet, current trends make it likely in the near future. Two bloody world wars in the early 20th Century gave birth to the United Nations. And global institutions, such as the International Court of Justice, continue to grow in both power and influence.

Conflict due to borders, cultural differences, and competing interests is waning due to increased travel and the advancement of technology. The interconnectedness of the global economy also decreases the
likelihood of war and increases the likelihood cooperation. Add in the
breakdown of language and communication barriers, and we're moving
closer and closer to a day when all the nations of the world unite in
common purpose.

10) **The Gospel of Jesus Preached Everywhere** – As you read this, the
Good News of Jesus Christ spreads across the planet like wildfire.
Television networks, websites, eBooks, YouTube videos, churches and
missionaries. Every medium and method you can think of feeds the
Gospel to a hungry planet.

Think about how rare this is. What are the odds of a first century
Israeli carpenter spreading His teachings to the whole world? Not good.
In fact, those are "long shot" odds. Yet we see it happening right now,
and Jesus said when it does, "the end will come."

CONVERGING SIGNS

But even in the midst of all these signs, one sign of the Second Coming is
bigger than any of the individual signs we've looked at so far. And what is
that sign? It's the convergence of all these signs.

Think about it. What are the odds of all these signs coming together
at one time? If the odds are a mere 1 in 10 for each of these signs, the odds
of them all occurring simultaneously is 1 in 10 billion!

Did one out of every ten first century spiritual leaders manage to spread
his message to the farthest corners of the globe? Has every generation had a
one in ten chance of witnessing the unification of Europe? The restoration
of Israel? A Russian-Iranian alliance? Of course not. These are all significant
signs.

And keep in mind, these signs don't include the fulfillment of "signs
within the signs" such as:

1) **Israel Reborn in a Single Day** – Isaiah predicted the rebirth of Israel in a single day. God Himself said Israel will be like a woman "who gives birth in an instant without labor pains" (*Isaiah 66:7-9*). And guess what? The nation of Israel was restored in a single day.

   On May 14, 1948, the Jewish People's Council issued an Israeli Declaration of Independence. The United States formally recognized the Jewish state *that same day*. Coincidence?

2) **Israel and Judah Unified** – Isaiah predicted the unification of Israel and Judah when God brings His people back into the land (*Isaiah 11:13*). The prophet Ezekiel agreed, saying Israel will be one kingdom, no longer divided (*Ezekiel 37:22*). Is this what we see?

   Yes. The state of Israel remains politically united as one nation with a unified government. And it's been this way since May 1948.

3) **Israel's Thriving Agriculture** – Through Isaiah, God promised to bring the Jewish people back into the land of Israel. But He also promised Israel will blossom agriculturally and fill the whole world with its fruit (*Isaiah 27:6*). When? Just prior to the Second Coming. Is this what we see?

   Yes. Today, the tiny nation of Israel (a desert wasteland less than a century ago) is one of the world's leading fresh citrus producers and a net exporter of more than forty varieties of fruit.

4) **The IDF as a Great Army** – The prophet Ezekiel revealed the Jewish people would come to life and stand up as "a great army" (*Ezekiel 37:10*). Zechariah said Israel will be like a blazing fire among sheaves of grain, burning up the neighboring nations (*Zechariah 12:6*). Even the weakest soldier among them will be like David (*Zechariah 12:8*).

   And what have we seen since 1948? The Israeli Defense Force is one of the greatest military forces in the world. Despite being surrounded by a sea of hostile neighbors, Israel continues to survive and thrive against all odds.

5) **Jerusalem at the Center of World Conflict** – God promised to make Jerusalem and Israel the center of world affairs in the last days. In fact, He said Jerusalem would be "an intoxicating drink" for the many

nations who send their armies against Jerusalem and Judah (*Zechariah 12:2-3*).

What do we see today? Israel and Jerusalem are a constant source of international turmoil. If the surrounding nations aren't actively attacking Israel, they're preparing for war and threatening war. Meanwhile, world diplomats are constantly drafting plans to divide Jerusalem and Judah in exchange for promises of peace.

6) **A Rebuilt Jewish Temple** – No, the Jewish Temple hasn't been rebuilt. But it will be. How can I be so sure? Because both Jesus and Daniel say the Antichrist will defile the Temple before the Second Coming. And how can this happen if the Temple doesn't exist? It can't. And that's exactly why you can count on seeing a news headline in the near future announcing plans to rebuild it.

The Romans destroyed the last Jewish Temple in A.D. 70. For the first time since then, we see groups such as the Temple Institute whose sole purpose is to rebuild the Temple. The Temple Institute is preparing priestly garments, musical instruments, and sacred vessels for the reestablishment of Old Testament Temple worship.

With the Jews in possession of Israel and Jerusalem, this possibility is more likely than in previous generations. So look for this to occur in the near future. What will lead to the construction of a third Temple? I don't know. Perhaps Israel's victory over the Gog of Magog alliance. No one will know until it happens. But if you're around when it does, remember that the Bible foretold it.

OTHER SIGNS

Each and every one of the signs mentioned so far is either fulfilled in our time or is in the early phases of fulfillment. But they aren't the only signs. The Bible has a lot to say about the last days and the end times, and we see those signs as well.

PEOPLE IN THE LAST DAYS

What will people be like in the last days? Fortunately, we don't have to speculate because the Bible tells us. Jesus Himself says the last days will be days of rampant immorality. He compares them to "the days of Noah," when God flooded the world because He could no longer bear the sight of man's depravity (*Matthew 24:37*).

In a letter to Timothy, Paul provides more detail. He says people will show the following characteristics in the last days:

1) **Boastful and Proud / Lovers of Self** – In the last days, people will be boastful and proud (*2 Timothy 3:2*). What does it mean to be boastful and proud? It means people will be cocky and pompous. They'll have all the answers, and they'll hold nothing sacred. Do we see this today?

    We do. Pride is the great vice we hardly ever see in ourselves, but we universally detest in other people. And while pride has always been present in society, it's never been embraced the way it is today.

    The Bible also says that people in the last days will love themselves only (*2 Timothy 3:2*). Man's selfish nature will take center stage in the world. Do we see this today?

    We do. Today's culture champions self-absorbed behavior. Our society celebrates pride, arrogance, and self-exaltation in business leaders, politicians, athletes, and celebrities of all sorts. Many spiritual leaders promote the idea that human beings are gods, and we need to learn to release our god-like powers. This is no different than believing the lie Satan told in the Garden of Eden. To entice Eve, Satan told her, "Eat of the tree, and you will be like God" (*Genesis 3:4-5*).

2) **Indifference to Others** – Paul said the love of many will grow cold in the last days (*2 Timothy 3:3*). People will be unloving with hardened hearts. They will be harsh and unforgiving. Do we see this today?

    We do. Every year, abortion kills millions of babies. Mass shootings occur on a regular basis. Murder is commonplace. Road rage. Child abuse. Adultery. Indifference and callous disregard for others is widespread. I hesitate to say things can't get worse, because in all likelihood they will.

Need an example of how bad things are? In Georgia, a teenager robbed a woman at gunpoint. When she didn't hand over the money he wanted (because she didn't have any), the teenager shot her baby in the head. During the investigation, the shooter's own mother and several of his family members conspired to help him cover up the crime. Indifference toward others? You bet.

In fact, it's quite likely this is the first time you've ever heard about this heinous act. Think about that. If this crime had occurred in the early 20th Century, it would have dominated news stories for a decade. But today? Today, it doesn't even make the front page.

3) **Lovers of Money** – According to Paul, people in the last days will be lovers of money (**2 Timothy 3:2**). Money will be the idol they worship. Do we see any evidence of this today? Yes. All around us.

People seek fame and fortune rather than seeking God. They dream not of heaven, but of winning the lottery or landing a reality show. It seems like people today will do almost anything for money. They'll make fools of themselves. Some will even murder for it.

Several years ago, a pharmacist in Kansas City pled guilty to intentionally diluting medication for cancer patients. His stated motive? Greed.

A few years later, police arrested two elderly women for insurance fraud. Their scam? Taking out life insurance policies on homeless men, then killing them in what appeared to be hit-and-run accidents. The two women collected over two million dollars. The only known motive? Again, it was greed.

4) **Lovers of Pleasure** – People will also be lovers of pleasure (**2 Timothy 3:4**). Hedonism will be the favorite pastime. Is this what we see today? It is. How many times have you heard, "If it feels good, do it?" People today routinely live lives centered around the pursuit of pleasure. And they do so regardless of the consequences.

Just look at the sexual immorality that runs free in today's society.

What else but an obsessive pursuit of pleasure explains it? Illicit drugs are everywhere. Why? Because people love pleasure. They can't get enough, and they're always in pursuit of a new "high" – anything that promises to fill the emptiness in their lives.

If all this sounds familiar, it's no coincidence. It sounds like your local newscast, doesn't it? Violence and immorality are all around us.

Of course, these behaviors have always been around. But not since the flood have they been this bad. Our televisions feature programming that would make the citizens of Sodom and Gomorrah blush – degenerate programming that's beamed into millions of homes.

This is our society today. It's as though the whole world has gone mad. It's a world where people call good evil and evil good (*Isaiah 5:20*)

SPIRITUALITY IN THE LAST DAYS

What about the state of people's spiritual lives in the last days? The Bible reveals that as well. Here are a few things it mentions:

1) **Religious Hypocrites** – According to Paul, people in the last days will pretend to be religious, but they will deny the power of God (*2 Timothy 3:5*). Do we see this today?

    We do. How many people do you know who go to church on Sunday, but live lives utterly devoid of God for the rest of the week. I'm not talking about people who don't live perfect lives. None of us live perfect lives. But we should at least try. We should focus on Christ. We should repent of our sins. How many people who claim to be Christians don't even think about Christ except in the church pew?

2) **Deniers of Creationism** – Jesus said that the last days will be just like the days of Noah (*Matthew 24:37*), and Paul tell us that in the days of Noah, people denied God's creation (*Romans 1:18-22*). Despite the fact that the earth, the sky, and all of nature scream out in testimony

of God's power – people in the last days will refuse to worship God or give Him credit for creation.

Do we see this today?

Yes. Today, many people place their faith in the big bang theory and the idea that human life (and all life in general) evolved as a result of random chance. Despite their inability to prove these claims, they cite these ideas as "facts" and mock the idea of God's existence. Often, anyone who expresses belief in God as Creator of the Universe is ridiculed as unenlightened – an intellectual lightweight.

3) **Deniers of the Second Coming** – According to Peter, people will deny the Second Coming in the last days (**2 Peter 3:3-4**). Not only will they dismiss it, they'll make fun of those who patiently await His return. They'll say things like, "*Jesus is coming, huh? You Christians have said that for 2,000 years now. But century after century, the world moves on just as it always has. When are you going to learn that's it's not going to happen?*"

To such people, the Second Coming (and God Himself) are fairy tales invented as escape mechanisms for people who have trouble coping with life.

Do we see this today? Yes. We do. Don't believe me? Then try this experiment. Tomorrow, tell everyone you meet how excited you are about the Second Coming of Jesus Christ and see what the reaction is. How many people do you think will share in your excitement? How many do you think will look at you like you're a lunatic?

4) **False Faith/Apostasy** – Paul told Timothy that in the last days people will reject the truth in favor of their own ideas. And they will seek out teachers who tell them what they want to hear (**2 Timothy 4:3-4**). In other words, many Christians will be Christians in name only. Their faith will be false, and they will reject the very religious beliefs they claim to believe.

Do we see this today? We do. News stories are filled with quotes from countless pastors, ministers, and priests who say the Bible isn't God's Word, that the blood of Jesus is not necessary for salvation.

5) **Occult Practices** – The Bible says that in the last days people will turn away from the true Christian faith. They will follow demonic teachings and cults will proliferate (*1 Timothy 4:1*).

Do we see this today? Yes. Some experts estimate the number of Christian cults at more than 1,600. A recent example of such a cult is the Fundamentalist Church of Jesus Christ of Latter-Day Saints (FLDS church). In 2006, the FBI put Warren Jeffs (FLDS church president) on its Most Wanted List. Authorities sought Jeffs on multiple charges of child sexual assault.

During the investigation, they found tape recordings of Jeffs using the name of Jesus to rape young girls. Did these revelations break his hold on the cult? No. The FLDS church remains intact to this day. And even though he's in a jail cell, Warren Jeffs continues to wield authority over his followers.

6) **False Messiahs** – According to Jesus, many false prophets will appear in the last days, deceiving many people (*Matthew 24:11*). Some of these false messiahs will come in the name of Jesus, claiming to be the Messiah (*Matthew 24:5*). Do we see this today? Unfortunately, yes.

In fact, the number of people led astray by false prophets and Messiahs in recent years is staggering. In 1978, Peoples Temple leader Jim Jones convinced more than 900 of his followers to drink cyanide-laced Kool-Aid in one of the largest mass suicides in history. In April 1993, Branch Davidian leader David Koresh, who claimed to be the Messiah, died in a fire along with 75 devoted followers. In March 1997, Heaven's Gate leader Marshall Applewhite convinced 38 followers to commit suicide with him – the largest mass suicide in U.S. history. And in 2007, Jose Luis De Jesus Miranda, a Miami man who claims to be Jesus, convinced his followers to tattoo 666 on their arms!

The signs of the Second Coming are all around us. According to Jesus, when we see these signs, it's an indication He's just around the corner. Do you think Jesus lied? Do you think He was mistaken? Of course not. God is always true to His Word. He gave us these signs because He wants us to look for them. Today, we see them.

"And when you see them," Jesus said. "Look up!" (***Luke 21:28***) Why? Because He's coming!

OUR GENERATION

Jesus likened the signs of His return to a fig tree. He said, "When you see the leaves sprout on a fig tree, you know without being told that summer is near. In the same way, when you see these signs, know that the Kingdom is near" (***Luke 21:29-33***).

So what did Jesus mean by this? He was saying that just as you know a budding fig tree is a sign that summer is on the way, you should also know He's about to return when you see the signs He described.

But Jesus was saying more than that. The fig tree is more than just an analogy. The blooming fig tree is a symbol of Israel. In the Old Testament, the fig tree was often used as a symbol for the nation of Israel. For example, God compared the people of Israel to ripe figs (***Hosea 9:10***), and He also compared the Babylonian exiles to good figs (***Jeremiah 24:5-7***).

So when Jesus cited the blooming of the fig tree as a sign of His return, He was saying the rebirth of Israel is a sign of a His return. In doing so, Jesus said ***the generation*** that witnesses the rebirth of Israel will not pass away until all these things take place (***Luke 21:32***). Did you catch that? According to Jesus, there's a generation alive today that will witness all the events of the Tribulation and the Second Coming.

But how long is a generation? Is it 20 or 40 years? How about 60? 80? 100? More? And even if there is a set number for a generation, when is the starting point for that generation? The Balfour Declaration (1917)? The restoration of Israel as a nation (1948)? The repossession of Jerusalem following the Six Day War (1967)? Regardless of the starting point or the exact measure of a generation, the time of His return is soon – within the expected lifetime of many people alive today.

Jesus didn't say, "When you see all these things, look up! Because I'm coming in a few hundred years!" He said, "Look up, because I'm coming *now*!"

CONCLUSION

Think about it. What are the odds of witnessing the simultaneous fulfillment or near fulfillment of all of these prophecies? Do you really believe it's just a coincidence? Do you really believe it's random chance? All these signs appear together in our time after 2,000 years of non-existence. Do you really think the world today is "the same as it's always been?" I don't. And you shouldn't either.

"But Britt," you say. *"What does it matter? Yes, you've convinced me these things are beyond coincidence. Jesus is coming. But so what? Why should I spend so much time obsessing over the Second Coming? Shouldn't I be focused on God's work?"*

You should, and this *is* God's work. Jesus commanded us to stay awake (*Mark 13:33-37*), and there's a reason. So if you don't already know why the Second Coming is so important, it's vital you find out. Fortunately, you don't have to make any guesses. The Bible tells you exactly why it matters.

CHAPTER 14
WHY DOES IT MATTER?

I T WAS LATE at night in the garden of Gethsemane. Jesus prayed, overcome with such grief His sweat fell to the ground as drops of blood. "Father," He said. "If you are willing, take this cup of suffering away from me. But let your will be done." Then Jesus stood up and returned to the disciples (*Luke 22:41-45*).

Earlier, He commanded them to keep watch. But now? They were asleep.

"Why are you asleep?" he asked. "Couldn't you stay awake for even one hour? Get up and pray so you will not fall into temptation" (*Matthew 26:40-41*). Minutes later, Judas betrayed Jesus into the hands of His enemies.

That evening, Jesus asked the disciples to do two things and two things only. Watch and pray. Yet what did the disciples do? They fell asleep.

Do you think they would've behaved differently if they had known what was about to happen? If they had known what the night would bring, do you think they would've stayed awake?

I do. Because when you expect something to happen, it changes the way you live. For example, let's say your doctor tells you tomorrow you have only six months to live. If that happens, you'll probably make major changes in the way you live your life – even if you end up living longer than six months. Likewise, if the disciples really believed the betrayal of Jesus was imminent, they would never have fallen asleep.

Do you see now why the Second Coming prophecies are so important? If you believe Jesus when He says He could return at any moment (and you should), then the impact on your life is dramatic. It's similar to the patient who hears he's got six months to live. If you believe Jesus could show up *tomorrow*, you live a far different life *today*.

It's All About Jesus

Despite the presence of so many signs, those who believe the Second Coming is near are often mocked and ridiculed. And I'm sad to say that many times that ridicule comes from fellow Christians. *"Why study all this prophecy?"* they say. *"If it's going to happen, it's going to happen. You should focus on God's work."*

But I ask, what better describes God's work than the study of bible prophecy? Or patiently waiting for the Second Coming? Jesus promised to return, and the heart of the Gospel is sharing that promise with others.

After all, the whole purpose of bible prophecy, *all of it*, is to give a clear witness to Jesus (*Revelation 19:10*). By some estimates, 25% of the Bible was prophecy when written. So if bible prophecy isn't important, then you can disregard one quarter of the Bible. Does that sound right to you? Of course not. The study of bible prophecy is the study of Jesus, and when you learn more about Jesus, you build a more intimate relationship with Him.

But there's another reason Christians should study the Second Coming prophecies: Jesus commanded us to. Jesus told His followers to watch and pray, not just in the Garden of Gethsemane, but right up until the day of His glorious appearing (*Mark 13:35-36*). Diligent prayer and watchfulness are critical elements in a Christian's life. Why? As I said before, when you watch and pray for the Second Coming, you live a different life.

Watch

What does it means to "watch"? If we made a list of activities we would expect Christians to engage in, "watchfulness" probably wouldn't top the list. In fact, most people wouldn't even think to add it to the list at all. But Jesus says it's a crucial aspect of Christian life. In fact, Jesus has a lot to say about how you should prepare for His return. Don't believe me? Just read the following parables:

The Parable of the Ten Bridesmaids – In this story (*Matthew 25:1-13*), Jesus tells about ten bridesmaids who took their lamps and went out to meet the bridegroom. Five were wise, and five were foolish.

The five wise bridesmaids brought extra oil for their lamps, while the five foolish ones didn't. When the bridegroom delayed His arrival, they all fell asleep. But they soon awoke to a shout that the bridegroom was coming. All ten gathered their lamps, but the five foolish bridesmaids realized their lamps were running out of oil.

"Give us some of yours," they demanded.

"We would," said the other five. "But if we did, we would run out of oil ourselves. Go buy your own."

So the five foolish bridesmaids left to go buy some oil. While they were gone, the bridegroom arrived. The wise five who were ready went with Him into the wedding feast and the door was locked behind them. When the others returned, they found the door locked. They pounded on the door and shouted, "Let us in." But the bridegroom responded, "I don't even know you!"

So what's the lesson here? We don't have to guess, because Jesus tells us. "Keep watch!" He says, "Because I could return at any moment" (*Matthew 25:13*). If you're wise, you'll be prepared to meet Jesus at all times. So prepare yourself now, because you don't know when He'll come.

The Parable of the Thief in the Night – In another parable, Jesus tells the story of a thief who breaks into a house under the cover of darkness. And He tells the disciples this: If you knew the exact moment when a thief was coming, you would keep watch over your house and not let the thief break in (*Luke 12:39-40*).

What's the point of this story? It's this: Keep watch and be ready at all times, otherwise Jesus will come when you least expect it (*Matthew 24:42-44*).

The Parable of the Master and His Servants – In this story, Jesus tells of a man who goes on a long trip and leaves one of his servants in charge of his household. This represents Jesus leaving us in charge of His affairs while He goes away for a time (in between His First and Second Comings).

Jesus said if the master returns and finds the servant acted faithfully, he'll give the servant a reward. But if the servant thinks to himself, "My master is leaving for a long time," and he spends his time eating, drinking, partying, and abusing his fellow servants, then he's in trouble. Because when the master returns unannounced, he'll kill the servant (*Luke 12:42-46*). That's why Jesus says we're blessed if He finds us *watching* when He returns (*Luke 12:35-36*)

Here we see that, once again, Jesus commands us to "watch." He warns against conforming to the ways of this world and the worries of this life. And how does He expect you to do this? By staying spiritually alert so the day of His return won't catch you like a trap. Jesus says a faithful servant lives life expecting His return at any moment (*Luke 12:35-38*).

Over and over again, Jesus says, "Watch! Don't let me find you asleep when I come back without warning" (*Mark 13:35-37*). This is a clear command. But what does it mean? It means Jesus can return at any moment, and He'll return without warning. After all, the rapture is a "sign-less" event. It could happen at any time. Nothing needs to happen first.

But the Second Coming? That's a different story. Signs will precede it. And Jesus expects us to recognize those signs. If He didn't, why would He command us to watch? He wouldn't, because we would have nothing to look for.

But when He says to "watch," Jesus means more than simply looking for the signs of His return. The writer of Hebrews puts it this way. He says "you should *eagerly await* the Second Coming of Jesus" (*Hebrews 9:28*). Now, do "await" and "watch" mean you should lay around staring at the walls and waiting for Jesus to come back? Do they mean you should climb the nearest hilltop and sit like the Millerites? No. That's not what Jesus has in mind.

Instead, He's saying you should constantly be "on guard." You should constantly be mindful of your relationship with Him so it remains strong. He's telling you to be alert so you don't get spiritually lazy. He's saying you should live every day of your life as if He could return at any moment. Do that, and your passion for Him will never fade.

And when you live your life with the constant expectation that Jesus could return at any moment, it produces at least two things. And those two things transform your life and the lives of those around you. So what are those two things?

Righteous living and a burning desire to share the Gospel.

LIVING A HOLY LIFE

Jesus says if you watch for Him, you're blessed. By preparing for His return, you won't be ashamed when He arrives. Because Jesus knows that, like the patient given six months to live, if you believe He's coming, you'll do your best to live a holy life (***Revelation 16:15***). In other words, belief in the nearness of His return is excellent motivation for living a life in harmony with God. Peter reinforces this idea. He says while waiting for Jesus to return, you should make every effort to live a blameless life in His sight (***2 Peter 3:14***).

If you believe in the Second Coming prophecies, as well as the command of Jesus to stay awake and alert, it will literally change your life. According to Paul, by looking forward to the Second Coming, you'll live a life of devotion to God, a life tempered with self-control and right conduct (***Titus 2:11-13***). Paul confirmed this in his letter to the Romans, when he encouraged the church to wake up and pursue righteous living. His stated reason? Because "it's late and time is running out" (***Romans 13:11***).

Study of the Second Coming prophecies fosters patience as well. Remember Peter's prophecy? He said in the last days scoffers will mock and ridicule those who eagerly await the Second Coming (***2 Peter 3:3-4***). We see these scoffers everywhere today. Enduring their ridicule will strengthen you, because certainty in the Second Coming gives you the patience and endurance to live by faith (*Hebrews 10:37*). Just as farmers look forward to the spring and summer rain, patiently waiting for the harvest to ripen, you too will learn to be patient as you look forward to His return (*James 5:7-8*).

Knowing that the things of this world will pass away, it only makes sense to live a holy life, looking forward to His return (*2 Peter 3:11-12*). Fulfilled prophecy is a constant reminder of God's awesome power, the glory of Jesus Christ, and the absolute certainty that promises yet fulfilled will come true.

SHARING THE GOSPEL

But when you live your life as if Jesus will return at any moment, righteous living isn't the only benefit. When you live this way, you're also compelled to share the Gospel. Why? Because you fully realize the urgency of sharing the Good News of Jesus with others.

For nearly 2,000 years, belief in the imminent return of Jesus has fueled this urgency. Today, that urgency is even greater. Why do I say that? Because the signs we see today should set the Christian church on fire. They tell us that the day of the Second Coming is fast approaching. And since the rapture precedes the Second Coming, that means the day of the rapture is even closer!

In our urgency to share the Gospel, it's important to know what a critical tool bible prophecy is. It provides strong evidence that God is the true author of the Bible. In fact, in the early days of the Church, bible prophecy was the *primary method* for spreading the Gospel. Don't believe me? Just read the New Testament.

On the day of Pentecost, Peter gave a rousing speech in Jerusalem where he cited fulfilled bible prophecy as evidence that Jesus is the long awaited Messiah (*Acts 2:14-42*). In fact, he told the crowd, "You are all witnesses" to the fulfillment of the Messianic prophecies (*Acts 2:32*). Did his argument work? According to the Bible, *yes*. Peter's speech led three thousand people to commit their lives to Jesus.

Later in the same book, Philip encounters an Ethiopian eunuch riding in a carriage. The eunuch is reading Isaiah 53:7-8 (a Messianic prophecy), but he doesn't understand what he's reading. Philip interprets the passage, and explains the Good News of Jesus. The result? The eunuch immediately believes and is baptized (*Acts 8:26-40*).

But Peter and Philip were not alone. Paul routinely used the Messianic prophecies to spread the Gospel everywhere he went. The following passage indicates the methods he used:

> *"As was Paul's custom, he went to the synagogue service, and for three Sabbaths in a row he used the Scriptures to reason with the people. He explained the prophecies and proved that the Messiah must suffer and rise from the dead. He said, 'This Jesus I'm telling you about is the Messiah'."* **Acts 17:2-3 (NLT)**

Notice the phrase, "as was Paul's custom." It's clear that this wasn't a one-time act. Instead, this was Paul's typical method for preaching the Gospel. And what was his method? He "used the scriptures to reason with the people," "explained the prophecies," and proved that Jesus was the Messiah. Paul used this same method earlier in Antioch of Pisidia. There, he entered a synagogue and preached that the condemnation and crucifixion of Jesus "fulfilled the prophets' words" and "all that the prophecies said about him" (*Acts 13:27-31*).

When Paul and Silas visited the synagogue in Berea, the Bible tells us that the people there listened to them. Then, they searched the scriptures day and night to see if what Paul and Silas were telling them was true (*Acts 17:10-12*). Did you catch that? They searched the scriptures to verify what Paul and Silas were teaching. And there's only one reason. Paul and Silas were teaching that Jesus fulfilled the Messianic prophecies, that Jesus was and is the Messiah.

Over and over again, the Bible tells us that Paul "testified that Jesus is the Messiah" (*Acts 18:5*). And Paul himself said, "I teach nothing except what the prophets and Moses said would happen" *Acts 26:22* (NLT). And when making the case for Jesus as Messiah, Paul asked King Agrippa, "Do you believe the prophets?" ***Acts 26:27*** (NLT). The Bible then tells us that, using the Law of Moses and the words of the prophets, Paul tried to persuade them about Jesus from the scriptures (***Acts 28:23-24***).

Fulfilled bible prophecy makes a powerful case for Jesus Christ. The Bible says the words of the prophets are a light shining in a dark place (***2 Peter 1:16-19***), and the signs we see today are a tool for spreading the Gospel. Why do I say this? Because raising awareness of the signs we see today can make a big difference in the lives of others. It might be the proof some people need in order to believe. Seeing firsthand fulfillment of bible prophecy in our time is just as compelling today as it was for the crowd on Pentecost and the Ethiopian eunuch almost 2,000 years ago.

THE COMING DAY OF JUDGMENT

We live in a world that thinks wisdom is foolishness and foolishness is wisdom (***1 Corinthians 3:18-19***). Is it any wonder then that society mocks those who look forward to the Second Coming?

If pressed, many of those same scoffers will say Jesus was a "good teacher." Yet Jesus commanded His followers to watch for His return. If He's not coming, is that really the mark of someone "good"? Of course not.

Despite what the critics say, watching for His return is extremely beneficial. A careful study of the Second Coming prophecies is important. These prophecies serve as a wake-up call to those who are captive to the temptations of this world. They motivate Christians to holy living and communicate the urgency of salvation to non-Christians. Paul made this clear in his letter to Titus, when he said you should "live in this fallen world with wisdom, righteousness, and devotion to God, while looking forward to the day when the glory of Jesus will be revealed." (***Titus 2:12-13***)

The Second Coming prophecies are not hidden. They're easy to understand for all Christians. And given the Bible's perfect track record when it comes to fulfilled prophecy, you should expect nothing less than the precise fulfillment of all the Second Coming prophecies as well. According to the signs, fulfillment of those prophecies is close at hand. Jesus is coming!

CHAPTER 15

HE'S COMING!

I N MY BOOK *Coming To Jesus: One Man's Search for Truth and Life Purpose*, I tell the story of my own struggle with the universal questions of life and how I began a personal search to uncover the truth. That search led me to the Bible, where I discovered the existence of countless specific and fulfilled prophecies. In my mind, these prophecies verified the authenticity of the Bible as nothing less than God's Word.

But I found something else – an entire subset of unfulfilled prophecies concerning the Second Coming of Jesus Christ and the seven year period just prior to His return. This book, of course, focused on those prophecies – and more specifically, the signs of His return.

But what if you don't believe in Jesus? Maybe you don't agree with me when I say that Jesus is God in the flesh. Or that the Bible is the Word of God. And I understand that. You want evidence, right? I know because I was once where you are. I wanted evidence, and I found it. I found that evidence in the Old Testament Messianic prophecies – prophecies fulfilled in the life, death, and resurrection of Jesus Christ. If you aren't familiar with those prophecies, I encourage you to examine them for yourself. I'm confident that if you do, you'll arrive at the same conclusion I have – that Jesus is the Messiah.

But I would also argue that the signs outlined in this book are their own evidence. If the Messianic prophecies don't convince you. If creation doesn't convince you. If the ministry of Jesus Himself doesn't convince you. If the testimony of the apostles doesn't convince you, then I hope visible signs of Second Coming prophecies fulfilled in your own day and time will convince you.

Nearly 2,000 years ago, Jesus triumphantly entered Jerusalem on the back of a donkey. Crowds threw their garments before Him and praised Him as the Messiah. This upset the religious leaders. "Teacher," they said. "Rebuke your followers!" But Jesus did no such thing. He said, "I tell you if they don't sing my praises, the very stones will cry out in my name" (*Luke 19:36-40*).

Today, the signs around us reveal the nearness of His return, and those signs cry out in testimony to Jesus. They call for you to come to Him now.

WHY YOU NEED JESUS

"But why?" you might say. *"Why do I need to come to Him? Why do I need Jesus?"* Because according to the Bible, we've all sinned and fallen short of the glory of God (*Romans 3:23*). And that presents a problem. Because God doesn't allow sinners into heaven.

In fact, the Bible says God's standard for entry into heaven is perfection (*Matthew 5:48*). Even if you're better behaved than most people, do you live up to *that* standard? Would you describe yourself as perfect?

Let me ask you this. Have you ever told a lie? If so, you broke God's 9th commandment (*Exodus 20:16*). Have you ever taken something that didn't belong to you? If so, you broke God's 8th commandment (*Exodus 20:15*). And the Bible says if you break one of God's laws, you're guilty of breaking them all (*James 2:10*).

If you answered yes to either of those questions, you're a sinner. In fact, Jesus says if you've ever lusted in your heart, you're guilty of adultery (*Matthew 5:28*). So don't delude yourself. By that standard, you're a sinner, I'm a sinner, and so is everyone else. And the Bible says the penalty for sin is death and eternal separation from God (*Romans 6:23*).

So if the standard that God uses to judge you is moral perfection, how do you think you'll measure up? Think you'll fall short?

"But Britt," you might say. *"Look at all my good deeds. Surely God won't overlook those."*

That's true. You can perform a lot of good deeds. You can feed the homeless, give all your money to charity, and teach orphan children to read and write. But you know what? All of those good deeds and a thousand more can't do one thing to erase a single sin from your life. When all is said and done, you'll still be guilty. And if God judges you guilty, do you really think heaven is your destination?

So what can you do? On your own – **nothing**. But don't let that depress you. You're not on your own. One man **did** live a life free of sin. That man was Jesus. And the Bible says Jesus paid the price for the sins of the world (*1 Peter 1:18-20*). He already paid for your sins and mine!

Jesus gave His life. His precious blood was shed on the cross for us. It's a free gift, and through God's grace, this free gift saves you, me, and everyone else who accepts it. How? By trusting that Jesus paid the penalty for our sin.

The Bible says Jesus was crucified for our sin, that He was whipped and beaten so we may be healed (*Isaiah 53:5*). Because of this, the Bible says there is no judgment for anyone who believes in Him. But for those who refuse to believe, they are judged already, because they rejected God's one and only Son (*John 3:18*).

Where do you stand with Jesus? If you don't know for sure, you need to find out **right now**. Why? Because the Bible not only says that Jesus is coming. It also says He's coming in judgment.

JUDGMENT DAY

That's right. The same Bible that said the Messiah would pour out His life as a sacrifice for others says He will return in judgment (*2 Corinthians 5:10*).

So regardless of whether Jesus comes tomorrow or many years from now, you will one day stand before Him in judgment. And on that day, Jesus said you are either for Him or against Him (*Matthew 12:30*). There's no in between. Are you ready for that day?

The Bible says that on Judgment Day, the earth and sky will flee His presence, and the Book of Life will be opened. It also says if your name is not found in that book, you'll be thrown into the lake of fire (***Revelation 20:11-15***). In the face of hundreds of fulfilled prophecies proving the Bible is the Word of God, are you willing to risk your soul on the idea that ***this time***, the Bible is wrong? If so, why? Is it pride? The Bible says pride goes before destruction (***Proverbs 16:18***). Don't let pride stop you from accepting Jesus right now.

The Bible says today is the day of salvation (**2 *Corinthians 6:2***). Not tomorrow or next year. ***Now***. You need to make sure your name is in the Book of Life, and you need to do that today.

So how do you do that? If you want, you can do it right now. All you have to do is say this prayer with a sincere heart:

"Dear Jesus, have mercy on my soul, for I am a sinner. I repent of my sins, and I believe that you died on the cross as forgiveness for my sins. I invite you to come into my life. Fill my heart with your Spirit, and I will trust and follow you as my Lord and Savior. In the name of Jesus. Amen."

Say that prayer, and your sins are forgiven. The Bible says, all who call on the name of the Lord will be saved (***Romans 10:13***).

THE SIGNS OF THE TIMES

Whether you believe Jesus will return or not, I think you'll agree when I say that the "things are the same as they've always been" argument is simply not true. Things aren't the same. They're dramatically different for our generation, and they promise to be far different with each passing year.

The signs point to our day and time as the season of Christ's return. Are you ready? If Jesus Christ comes tomorrow, are you ready? Even if He doesn't, tomorrow could still be your last day on earth. You can die in any number of ways.

You could have a heart attack. You could die in a traffic accident. Do you know how many people die on the road every year? It's a lot. No matter how smart, rich, or well-connected you are, you can't be sure tomorrow isn't your last day. You don't have the slightest bit of control over it.

Tomorrow could be the day you come face-to-face with Jesus. Are you ready if it is? Do you have a personal relationship with Him? If not, I encourage you to begin that relationship today. Time is running short. He's coming. The Bible says so, and if I were you, I wouldn't bet against the Bible.

Remember, the same Bible said Jesus would be betrayed for the exact sum of 30 pieces of silver (*Zechariah 11:12*). It said the modern state of Israel would be born in a single day (*Isaiah 66:7-8*). It said God would bring the Jews back into the land of Israel from among all the nations where He had exiled them (*Jeremiah 16:14-15*). And the same Bible says that Jesus is coming in our expected lifetime (*Matthew 24:34*).

Don't forget, when Jesus first came, the religious leaders failed to recognize the signs of His coming. And many of the people who witnessed the miracles of Jesus refused to believe in Him because they put their faith in the religious leaders. And those leaders did not believe in Jesus.

In similar fashion, many of today's Christian leaders dismiss the signs of the Second Coming. Will history repeat itself? Will people simply accept what those leaders say instead of reading the Bible for themselves? I hope not.

If you're a Christian, my hope is that you will rely on the Bible for instruction and not the wisdom of men. Jesus says if a blind man leads another blind man, they will both fall in a ditch (*Luke 6:39*). But don't take my word for it. Take your direction from God Himself. Study His Word, and listen to the Holy Spirit.

When I say Jesus will return in our generation, don't accept or reject that until you investigate for yourself. Study the Second Coming prophecies and ask God to give you insight into the truth.

In studying those prophecies, turn to the last words in the last chapter of the last book in the Bible. In it, Jesus declares no less than three times, "I am coming soon!" (*Revelation 22:7,12,20*). And I can't think of a better way for this book to end than by repeating His promise:

> *"Look, I am coming soon, bringing my reward with me to repay all people according to their deeds. I am the Alpha and the Omega, the First and the Last, the Beginning and the End"*
>
> ***Revelation 22:12-13 (NLT).***

Amen! Come, Lord Jesus. Come.

ABOUT THE AUTHOR

Britt Gillette is a devoted follower of Jesus Christ, husband to Jen, and father to Samantha and Tommy. He and his family live in Virginia. He's also the author of:

Coming To Jesus: One Man's Search for Truth and Life Purpose

If you want to receive an automatic email when Britt's next book is released, please sign up on his website. Your email address will never be shared and you can unsubscribe at any time.

SPREAD THE WORD

Word-of-mouth is crucial for any book to succeed. If you enjoyed this book, please consider leaving a review at Amazon. Even if it's only a sentence or two, it would make a world of difference and would be very much appreciated.

Also, please consider using social media to share this book with others. Tell your Facebook friends, your Twitter followers, and others. You can make a difference in someone's life today by sharing the Good News of Jesus Christ.

COME VISIT US ON THE WEB

Britt writes a number of articles about Jesus Christ and bible prophecy on his website, www.end-times-bible-prophecy.com. Please drop by and visit!

Made in the USA
Columbia, SC
31 December 2020